Prisons and Forced Labour in Japan

Prisons and Forced Labour in Japan examines the local, national and international significance of convict labour during the colonization of Hokkaido between 1881 and 1894 and the building of the Japanese empire.

Based on the analysis of archival sources such as prison yearbooks and letters, as well as other eyewitness accounts, this book uses a framework of global prison studies to trace the historical origins of prisons and forced labour in early modern Japan. It explores the institutionalization of convict labour on Hokkaido against the backdrop of political uprisings during the Meiji period. In so doing, it argues that although Japan tried to implement Western ideas of the prison as a total institution, the concrete reality of the prison differed from theoretical concepts. In particular, the boundaries between prisons and their environment were not clearly marked during the colonization of Hokkaido.

This book provides an important contribution to the historiography of Meiji Japan and Hokkaido and to the global study of prisons and forced labour in general. As such, it will be useful to students and scholars of Japanese, Asian and labour history.

Pia Maria Jolliffe is a Research and Teaching Associate at the Nissan Institute of Japanese Studies and a Research Fellow at Blackfriars Hall, University of Oxford, UK. She is the author of *Learning, Migration and Intergenerational Relations: The Karen and the Gift of Education* (2016).

Routledge Focus on Asia

Prisons and Forced Labour in Japan

The Colonization of Hokkaido, 1881–1894

Pia Maria Jolliffe

Routledge
Taylor & Francis Group

LONDON AND NEW YORK

First published 2019
by Routledge
2 Park Square, Milton Park, Abingdon, Oxon OX14 4RN

and by Routledge
52 Vanderbilt Avenue, New York, NY 10017

First issued in paperback 2020

Routledge is an imprint of the Taylor & Francis Group, an informa business

British Library Cataloguing-in-Publication Data
A catalogue record for this book is available from the British
Library

Library of Congress Cataloging-in-Publication Data
Names: Jolliffe, Pia, author.
Title: Prisons and forced labour in Japan : the colonization of
    Hokkaido, 1881–1894 / Pia Maria Jolliffe.
Description: Abingdon, Oxon ; New York, NY : Routledge, 2019. |
    Series: Routledge focus on Asia ; 3 | Includes bibliographical
    references and index.
Identifiers: LCCN 2018033056 | ISBN 9780815383208 (hardback) |
    ISBN 9781351206358 (ebook) | ISBN 9781351206334 (epub) |
    ISBN 9781351206327 (mobipocket encrypted)
Subjects: LCSH: Forced labor—Japan—Hokkaido—History—
    19th century. | Convict labor—Japan—Hokkaido—History—
    19th century. | Prisons—Japan—Hokkaido—History—19th
    century. | Hokkaido (Japan)—Colonization.
Classification: LCC HD4875.J3 J65 2019 | DDC
    331.11/730952409034—dc23
LC record available at https://lccn.loc.gov/2018033056

ISBN 13: 978-0-367-67040-5 (pbk)
ISBN 13: 978-0-8153-8320-8 (hbk)

Typeset in Times New Roman
by Apex CoVantage, LLC

To William, Joseph and Teresa

Contents

Illustrations

Technical notes

All Japanese terms have been transcribed according to the Hepburn romanization system. Japanese names of persons are given in the usual Japanese order: surname, then first name. Translations from foreign language texts and unit conversions are, unless otherwise noted, my own.

Acknowledgements

The original wish to carry out a study on the topic of prisons and forced labour in Japan came to life while I was doing an academic exchange year at Yokohama Shiritsu Daigaku (Yokohama City University), made possible by a Joint Study Scholarship from the University of Vienna. It was during this year that I visited Abashiri, a small city at the Sea of Okhotsk. Abashiri is known in Japan as a prison town. A prison museum provides visitors with information on the history and the stark living conditions of the Meiji-era prison. I was impressed by this history and decided to draft an in-depth research project on the topic of prison and forced labour in early modern Japan.

At the Institute for East Asia Studies at the University of Vienna, Sepp Linhart supervised my study with great interest from the very beginning, supporting me by asking important questions on the topic and giving me tips on the relevant literature. Stimulating questions from Wolfram Manzenreiter, Ina Hein, Ingrid Getreuer-Kargl, Roland Domenig and Bernhard Seidl, as well as their students, also contributed to the development of this work. I am particularly grateful for their invitation to present and discuss my work in the AAJ (Akademischer Arbeitskreis Japan) lecture series.

In the United States, Daniel Botsman (Yale University) generously shared his research expertise with me.

I gratefully acknowledge the Great Britain Sasakawa Foundation who offered me a grant to revisit Hokkaido for follow-up research at Hokkaido Daigaku (University of Hokkaido) in Sapporo. There, I benefitted from discussions with Philip Seaton and his students. I also thank the German Institute for Japanese Studies (DIJ Tokyo) for the opportunity to present my work to the DIJ History & Humanities Study Group.

At the Nissan Institute of Japanese Studies, University of Oxford, I wish to thank Sho Konishi, Alice Freeman and the members of the Japanese History Workshop for their collegial friendship, questions and critical remarks on my work-in-progress. I am grateful to Maro Dotulong for designing the maps in this study, to Chinami Oka and Kimiko Kuga for their research assistance and to Michelle Chew for proofreading the manuscript. Of course, all remaining mistakes are mine. Hugh Whittaker and Jane Baker supported me in the planning of this research, and Roger Goodman encouraged me to submit the manuscript to Routledge where Stephanie Rogers and Georgina Bishop provided helpful editorial assistance. I also express gratitude to three anonymous reviewers who commented on early versions of this book.

My family in Austria and the United Kingdom have been very supportive throughout this research. My parents Franz and Maria Vogler encouraged me from early on in my studies about Japan. I also thank my husband William Jolliffe for supporting my research on Japanese history and for travelling with me and our children to Japan. I am grateful for the joy their loving company adds to my work at home and abroad.

Oxford, September 2018

Map 0.1 Map of Japan with important sites of this study

(Map designed by Maro Dotulong)

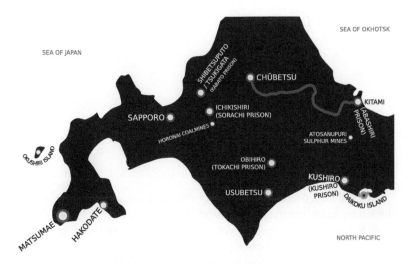

Map 0.2 Map of Hokkaido with important sites of forced prison labour
(Map designed by Maro Dotulong)

Foreword

Prisons and forced labour are unlikely to feature in many people's images of Hokkaido, Japan's northernmost island. The picture postcard image of Hokkaido today is of wide open spaces, specular scenery, adventure pursuits in the great outdoors, world-class powder snow for skiers, delicious cuisine, extensive agriculture and cool summers where people from the rest of Japan escape to in July and August. This is the popular image of Hokkaido today promoted in numerous documentaries, works of popular culture and tourism campaigns. But such images obscure the more complicated, contested and brutal history of Hokkaido, and its role in the formation of the modern Japanese state.

On the northern Okhotsk coast of Hokkaido, not far from the UNESCO World Natural Heritage Site in the Shiretoko Peninsula is the small city of Abashiri. Throughout Japan, the city is probably best known for being the site of a prison. Today there is a modern gaol in Abashiri, but the buildings of the former prison have also been preserved and have been open to the public as an open-air museum since 1983. The Abashiri Prison Museum is something of an anomaly. There are many prisons around the world which have become tourist sites, often as a memorial to important members of political movements or oppressed peoples who had been incarcerated there. Others are more akin to so-called "dark tourism" sites, which cater to people's macabre fascination with exhibitions about death, torture and suffering. However, the narrative of the Abashiri Prison Museum corresponds quite closely to what Michele Mason (2012) has called the "dominant narratives of colonial Hokkaido and imperial Japan". These romanticized narratives of "development" and the opening up of the land for settlement and cultivation in the Meiji Period (1868–1912) are prioritized over the often brutal and bloody forces that drove forward Japan's modernization and expansion in that period.

In early 2018, the text of the Abashiri Prison Museum visitor's pamphlet posted on the museum's website seems more appropriate for a stately home than a prison: the pamphlet is titled, "The Beauty of Hundred-Year-Old Buildings that are Important Cultural Properties". The detailed content of the pamphlet also contains positive, uplifting phrases. For example, the section on the background of the prison's construction is subtitled: "Road construction was the first step in the modern development of Hokkaido. It also marked the beginning of the history of Abashiri Prison". The museum's website and pamphlet focus visitors' initial attention on the architectural features of the buildings which have been designated nationally important cultural properties (particularly those built in the early 20th century) and on the progressive achievements of the prison system, in alignment with a positive narrative of development. It is only in the small print that the extreme hardship endured within the prison walls is depicted:

> In 1890, 50 prison inmates were moved from Kushiro Prison to Abashiri, where only 631 people had been living. Construction of the Abashiri Prison started. In the following year, 1,200 inmates were mobilized to build Central Road between Kitami and Abashiri. They built 163 km of road in just under 8 months. From harsh labor in extreme winter weather, 211 inmates died. To convey this history to coming generations, the museum opened in 1983 as one of the few outdoor historical museums in Japan.
>
> (Abashiri Prison Museum, n.d.)

When I visited Abashiri Prison Museum in 2008, I made sure it was during the coldest time of year in late January. Abashiri is on the same latitude as New York and northern Italy but has a subarctic climate. The northern coast of Hokkaido is the most southerly point in the northern hemisphere with annual sea ice. The ice floes are Abashiri's other main attraction and a potent symbol of how long and bitterly cold Hokkaido winters are, with snow on the ground for a third of the year and temperatures frequently dipping below -20 degrees Celsius. As I wandered through the wooden prison buildings, I could imagine just how brutal the winters would have been for the inmates who would have worn thin prison garments offering much less protection against the cold than my own heavy winter coat.

The museum thus offers only a selective view of the history of Abashiri Prison. In addition to the sanitization and "entertainmentization" which inevitably occurs to make the site more appealing as a tourist attraction, there is also a question of how representative Abashiri Prison was of prisons in Hokkaido overall. Despite being Hokkaido's most prominent prison in contemporary public imagination, Abashiri Prison was by no means the largest or most significant prison in Meiji Period Hokkaido. It served as one of five detention centres on Hokkaido – the others were in Kabato,

Sorachi, Kushiro and Tokachi – and was established as a branch of Kushiro Prison. However, Abashiri Prison has assumed the mantle of being the "representative" Hokkaido prison in the modern popular imagination both via its preservation as a tourist site and by becoming an icon within popular culture. For example, the actor Takakura Ken starred in a series of hit films in the 1960s and early 1970s titled *Abashiri Bangaichi* (Abashiri Prison); and in the road movie *Shiawase no kiiro hankachi* (Yellow Handkerchief of Happiness), he plays a miner released from prison in Abashiri who returns home to see if his wife is still waiting for him. Such works are not about the Meiji Period, but nevertheless link the town of Abashiri with prisons in the popular imagination. The combination of an uplifting dominant narrative of Hokkaido's development with a re-telling of Abashiri Prison history focusing on cultural importance and architectural beauty, which is alluded to in numerous works of popular entertainment, creates a specific image of prisons in Hokkaido. This image does not deny the brutal realities of life within the prison walls, but certainly sidelines that brutality in favour of more favourable elements of the historical narrative.

A challenge to this sanitization of the history of Hokkaido's prisons has come primarily from local historians working in what is called the people's history movement (*minshūshi undō*). The Okhotsk region of Hokkaido was a pioneer for this kind of research, which focuses on the voices of ordinary people, particularly the oppressed and victimized (see Oda, 2016). Prison labour was one of the early subjects examined by the people's history groups because the narratives were about events that had occurred in their own communities. Indeed, the road which cost so many lives of the Abashiri prisoners back in the 1890s is still the main transportation artery between Asahikawa and Abashiri that connects Hokkaido's central region with its northeast.

Now, thanks to Pia Maria Jolliffe's monograph, which builds upon and extends the work of local historians in Hokkaido, we have for the first time in English a detailed, nuanced and highly readable account of the prison system in Hokkaido and its role in the development of Hokkaido. She first sets the prison system within historical and geographical context, describing how prisons in Hokkaido emerged from both the practices of incarceration during the Edo period and the particular need for prisons in Hokkaido given the colonial policies of the Meiji State. By providing detailed analysis of the various prisons and the variations within their conditions for inmates, a picture emerges of the depths to which human existence may sink and the depth of resilience people may find to overcome such hardships. Through extensive engagement with the available primary sources, we hear the voices of inmates, the attitudes of their gaolers and the concerns of local communities who experienced a sudden influx of prisoners and guards into their midst. By drawing together international scholarship on the role and nature of prisons/punishment, histories of Hokkaido's colonization, and the Japanese primary sources, Dr Jolliffe shows us the complex history behind the more idealized and simplified version of the prison narrative as seen in popular culture representations or heritage sites such as the Abashiri Prison Museum. The result is a work that shines a light not only on a fascinating and formative moment of Hokkaido history, but also on the contrasts that frequently exist between the heritage that people would like to preserve in public consciousness or show to outside visitors, and the more complicated history that will not disappear while there are people dedicated to preserving the historical record.

Philip Seaton
Tokyo University of Foreign Studies

Bibliography

Abashiri Prison Museum (n.d.), *Visitor's Pamphlet (English)*. www.kangoku.jp/multilingual_english/english.pdf, accessed 2 May 2018.

Mason, M. 2012, *Dominant Narratives of Colonial Hokkaido and Imperial Japan*. London: Palgrave Macmillan.

Oda, H. 2016, Unearthing the History of *minshū* in Hokkaido: The Case Study of the Okhotsk People's History Workshop. In Seaton, P. ed. *Local History and War Memories in Hokkaido*. London: Routledge, pp. 129–158.

Introduction

This study starts with the assumption that the construction of prisons and the use of prisoners' work created the basis for the colonization of Hokkaido, and that these institutions, or rather their inmates' activities, therefore contributed to the economic development and industrialization of the modern Japanese Empire. In order to examine this assumption, the study is guided by two primary questions. Firstly, I am interested in the reason behind a total of five detention centres being built on Hokkaido from 1881 onwards, and whether it is possible to identify a correlation between the Meiji-era process of colonization on Hokkaido and the dynamics of convict labour. Secondly, after establishing a link between these two processes, I ask how this convict labour contributed concretely to the colonization of the northernmost Japanese island and of central Japan.

In this way, this study builds on and contributes to Meiji historiography and the history of the Japanese Empire in general, and the history of Ezo/ Hokkaido in particular. This study also adds to the study of the history of prisons and forced labour in Japan.

The book contributes to Meiji historiography as it questions the notion of the "opening of Japan" (Konishi, 2007) and thus departs from Western ideas of progress:

> Historians have rarely questioned one aspect of the birth of modern Japan: the 'Opening of the Nation' to the West, or *kaikoku*, and the resulting initiation of civilization and progress. As a result, the meaning of *kaikoku* has been closed, and alternative narratives of modern Japanese history have essentially been precluded from the historiography on Japan.
>
> (Konishi, 2007, p. 101)

Indeed, conventional Meiji historiography has typically focused on statesmen and presents the Meiji Restoration (Nagai and Urrutia, 1985) as a political and economic success story (Huffman, 2006). In recent decades, new places and spaces have entered Meiji historiography. For instance, scholarship has started to focus on new groups and individuals as agents of Meiji history. These agents share the characteristics that they are non-state actors such as women (Anderson, 2010; Steger, 1994; Walthall, 1998), indigenous peoples (lewallen, 2016a; Siddle, 1997) or religious (Burkman, 1974; Ketelaar, 1990; Scheiner, 1970). My own research conceives of "prisoners" as agents of Meiji history who through their forced labour have significantly contributed to the colonization and development of Japan's northernmost island of Hokkaido. In this way my research also contributes to a Meiji historiography decentred from Edo/Tokyo and the politically important *han* Chōshū and Satsuma. In this respect the work of the Japanese historian Amino Yoshihiko is very influential. Amino evidences the social construction of the nation known today as "Japan". His research draws attention to political and historical processes in areas that are generally considered "periphery", encouraging us to radically re-think conventional ideas of "centre" and "periphery" (Amino, 1992, 2000). Similarly, Tessa Morris-Suzuki (1994) discusses the various meanings of Japan's northern frontier, drawing attention to the different political meanings Ezo and the Ainu had for the *wajin*. Karen Wigen's (1995) case study of Shimona region sheds light on how during the Meiji Restoration many areas of Japan were redefined in both economic and social terms. Her geographical approach to history highlights the importance of space in processes of social transformation, which also allows us to discern the intersection of local and global power dynamics (Wigen, 1995).

The transformation from Ezo to Hokkaido was a long process that started well before the Meiji Restoration. Importantly, the geographical context of colonial Ezo/Hokkaido challenges predominant ideas of "the opening of Japan". Recent scholarship on early modern Ezo evidences ongoing cultural and economic exchanges between the Ainu inhabitants of Ezo and the *wajin* (Japanese) population (Howell, 2005; Morris-Suzuki, 1994; Siddle, 1996; Walker, 2001). Yet, as mentioned previously, conventional historiography is still shaped by a dominant narrative of the "opening of Japan" (Konishi, 2007), a process during which Hokkaido was merely "developed" economically. The next sections discuss Tokugawa and Meiji processes of the colonization of Ezo/Hokkaido.

The Tokugawa colonization of Ezo

Hokkaido's colonial status has long been neglected by colonial studies of the Japanese Empire (Mason, 2012; Seaton, 2017). In his analysis of the grand narratives of empire and development in Japan, Philip Seaton identifies two main narratives of empire: a dominant narrative and a critical counter-narrative (Seaton, 2016, p. 26).

The dominant narrative starts with Japan's annexation of Taiwan (1895) and subsequently includes Karafuto (annexed in 1905), Kwantung (leased in 1905), Korea (annexed in 1910) and the Nan'yo islands (leased in 1905), as well as the armed occupation of Manchuria in 1931 (Matsusaka, 2006). In this view, Ezo before 1855 is considered part of Japan's legitimate sphere of influence. Accordingly, the colonial status of Hokkaido as well as of Okinawa are routinely ignored (Christy, 1997, p. 142; Seaton, 2016, p. 28). For example, Beasley's (1987) study locates Japanese Imperialism between the years 1894 and 1945. Mark Peattie, author of the chapter "The Japanese Colonial Empire" in *The Cambridge History of Japan* notes that during the 1870s and 1880s Japan acquired nearby overseas territories such as the Bonin islands, the Ryūkyū Kingdom and the Kurile Islands. Although Peattie mentions that Japan was "strengthening its grip on Hokkaido through an intensified programme of colonization", he suggests that "this effort was less the initial step toward colonial expansion than it was a reassertion of national authority over territories traditionally within the Japanese cultural sphere" (Peattie, 2008, p. 224). Peattie goes on to claim that the actual colonization of these "no man's lands" was a mere "clarification of national boundaries" similar to processes of nation building in 19th- and 20th-century Europe (Peattie, 2008, p. 224). He also suggests that Japan's focus on Korea from the 1880s onwards was "Japan's first effort in modern times to exert influence, if not direct control over alien people" (Peattie, 2008, p. 224). This view completely ignores the Japanese expansion towards Ezo which started in the fourth and fifth centuries (Hudson, 2014, p. 131; Kreiner and Ölschleger, 1987, pp. 27–28).

Indeed, a critical counter-narrative to the dominant narrative argues that Japanese imperialism started before 1895. This counter-narrative emerged from within Hokkaido's local history activism and has been taken up by Western scholarship since the 1990s (Seaton, 2016, pp. 26–27). For example, Tessa Morris-Suzuki's work evidences how, long before the Meiji state's formal colonization of Ezo, "Tokugawa colonialism" (Morris-Suzuki, 1994, p. 2) exercised control over Ezo and its indigenous inhabitants, the Ainu. So, it was in Ezo that Japan's colonial policies were largely developed (Calman, 1992, p. 28; lewallen, 2016b, p. 60; Mason, 2012, pp. 4–5; Morris-Suzuki, 1995).

In contrast to other domains, the Matsumae *han*'s economy was not based on rice agriculture but on trade with the Ainu, where vassals received rights to trade with the Ainu at particular locations (*basho*). The resulting *basho*-system (*basho seido*) caused significant changes in the relations between Ainu and *wajin* (Japanese). In particular, the establishment of large-scale fisheries impacted on the Ainu's independent way of life as many of them became contractors and workers for Japanese tradespersons. In some areas the Ainu were also coerced into providing labour (Siddle, 1996, pp. 36–37). These economic changes additionally impacted social perceptions of the natural environment. Tessa Morris-Suzuki (2013) analyses the effect of felling forests during the colonization of Hokkaido and Karafuto from the late 17th century onwards. She explains how for the Ainu forests provided their livelihood as they typically contained all the natural resources necessary for the Ainu's subsistence economy. By contrast, the *wajin's* colonial perception of forests focused on the market value of trees, for example in the production of pulp and paper (Morris-Suzuki, 2013, pp. 238–239).

In terms of relations between the colonizers and colonized, the Matsumae *han* practiced a dissimilation policy that emphasized the Ainu's "otherness". However, between 1799 and 1821 when the shogunate perceived a threat arising from the Russian Empire, the *bakufu* put Ezo under its control and promoted the assimilation of the Ainu of Etorofu in order to secure *bakufu* sovereignty over the southern Kurils and remaining Ezo-chi. Importantly, Philip Seaton notes that "this placement of a foreign land under the direct rule of the political centre meets the definition of colonialism, although it is rarely referred to as such" (Seaton, 2017, p. 6).

This colonial assimilation policy was abandoned when the Russian threat subsided in the early 19th century. However, when the *bakufu* resumed more active relations with Western nations in the 1850s, the matter of defining a northern frontier of the Japanese nation state became a political priority. In 1855 the Kuril islands were assigned to Russia whilst the status of Sakhalin remained uncertain. As a consequence, the shogunate once more asserted direct administration of the northernmost island and implemented a large-scale assimilation policy on the Ainu. The objective was, again, to make the Ainu's Japanese identity visible in order to encourage international recognition of the Ainu's Japanese nationality. This, in turn, would justify Japan's claim for territorial rights to Ainu land located in the strategically important areas of Hokkaido, the Kuril islands and Southern Sakhalin. In 1875 the Kurils were indeed given to Japan. In exchange, Japan had to renounce sovereignty over Sakhalin (Morris-Suzuki, 1994, p. 9; Howell, 2005, p. 144).

This critical counter-narrative of empire and development demonstrates that Tokugawa colonialism in Ezo was an important antecedent to later forms of Japanese imperialism (Mason, 2012, p. 4; Morris-Suzuki, 1994, pp. 3–4; Seaton, 2016, p. 28).

The Meiji colonization of Hokkaido

The dominant narrative outlined previously has also shaped academic and popular discourses of Hokkaido's Meiji history. In this viewpoint, the

Japanese engaged in the settlement of empty land in Hokkaido after 1868 (Seaton, 2016, p. 28), so the official Japanese narrative neutrally describes Japanese activities on Hokkaido during the Meiji era as *kaitaku* (colonization or land development) instead of as *shokuminchika* (colonization). Several authors of the critical counter-narrative have problematized this terminology, arguing that *kaitaku* is a euphemism that masks processes of colonial appropriation of the indigenous Ainu's land: "Prevailing national narratives weave Hokkaido's complex and fraught history into a seamless tale of Japan's modernization that favours a lexicon of development (*kaitaku*) and progress (*shinpō*) over colonization and conquest" (Seaton, 2016, p. 52). The Japanese intellectual Komori Yōichi even calls the Meiji government's development plan for Hokkaido an "invasion in the name of development" (Komori, 2012, p. 64). He emphasizes that Ainu Moshir (the Ainu term for Ezo) was categorized as a no-man's land, and consequently claimed as Japanese territory (Komori, 2001, pp. 14–15). Indeed, this non-concession of territorial rights is a key point in colonial strategies: dispossessed of their land rights, indigenous peoples are unable to qualify as "states", which excludes them from qualifying as legal subjects under international law. This situation enables foreign states to claim the territories of indigenous people for themselves (Anaya, 1996, p. 19).

The Meiji Restoration clearly had a significant impact on the Tokugawa colonization of Ezo. During the Boshin War (*Boshin Sensō*), Hakodate became a central site when Admiral Enomoto Takeaki fled there with his anti-government forces. In the Battle of Hakodate (*Hakodate Sensō*) Enomoto's forces were quickly defeated, and on 27 June 1869 Ezo came under the rule of the Meiji government. Soon afterwards, on 15 August 1869, Ezo was renamed "Hokkaido" which literally translates as "northern sea route", a name which alludes to Japanese views of the island being a "northern gateway of the Japanese empire" (Oguma, 2017, p. 22).

A special Hokkaido Commission for Colonization (Kaitakushi) was then established. The government invested 4–5 per cent of its total budget in the Kaitakushi and in 1870 employed Kuroda Kiyotaka. Kuroda was originally from Satsuma, which was one of the political hot spots during the early days of the Meiji Restoration. He had studied military technology in Edo and was charged with the suppression of Enomoto's forces. At the Kaitakushi, Kuroda developed a 20-year plan for the economic development of Hokkaido (Irish, 2009, pp. 115–119). An immigration policy was also part of Kuroda's development plan, whereby the Kaitakushi promoted group immigration especially from Honshu. Between 1869 and 1871, 18 immigrant groups arrived in Hokkaido, 11 of whom consisted of former samurai while the remaining were commoners. Throughout the next 12 years an estimated 12,000 people emigrated to Hokkaido. Most of them were asked to settle in the Ishikari valley. The Kaitakushi provided them with financial aid for 3 years, but there were nevertheless considerable challenges to the immigrants adapting to the new way of life. The clearing of land, as well as the growing of wheat and other northern crops, was very difficult, not to mention the challenge of adapting to the new climate and isolation. For these reasons it was not easy to attract migrants to Hokkaido. Many of those who did migrate there returned to Honshu once the Kaitakushi's 3 years of support ended.

The *tondenhei* (farmer-soldiers) system was another effort by the Kaitakushi to recruit former samurai whose superiors had not supported the Meiji Restoration. These samurai were now impoverished and in need of new ways to provide for their livelihood. Thus, from 1874 onwards the Kaitakushi officially recruited *tondenhei*, and the following year 198 soldier farmers arrived with their families in Sapporo. Each former samurai received 8 acres of land and a house equipped with a Russian-style stove. Since the men agreed to provide military services, all those aged between 18 and 35 years received winter uniforms and participated in military exercises. As former samurai, they were also allowed to keep on wearing their swords and additionally received guns. The idea was for them to protect Hokkaido, and thus Japan's northern frontier, from any potential Russian threat (Irish, 2009, p. 119; Linhart, 1969, pp. 55–56). Importantly, these new groups of immigrants and *tondenhei* replaced the Ainu as a major colonial labour force (Hirano, 2017; Siddle, 1997, pp. 67–68).

The Kaitakushi was meant to operate only for 10 years, with the intention of dissolving in 1881. However, Kuroda Kiyotaka, who had been Head of the Kaitakushi since 1874, opposed this abolishment, worried that the development of the island would not proceed without the institution. However, he was unable to reverse the government's plan and the Kaitakushi was abolished in 1881 after a financial scandal involving Kuroda Kiyotaka was made public. Kuroda had put together a deal to sell Kaitakushi assets to officials for 1/36th of their costs. He argued this would make the Kaitakushi's projects sustainable. But when Tokyo agreed to this deal, political unrest erupted (Irish, 2009, p. 123).

After the dissolution of the Kaitakushi, its administrative responsibilities were transferred to three newly established prefectures (*ken*), Nemuro, Hakodate and Sapporo, from 1882 to 1886, which is why this period is also known as *san ken ikkyoku jidai* (time of three prefectures and a single office) in the literature (Enomoto, 1999, p. 239). Because the existing immigration policy proved not very successful, the Meiji government decided to establish prisons on Hokkaido. In this way, colonization would be accelerated by using the forced labour of thousands of convicts. In 1886 the Hokkaido-cho was created and the Meiji government appointed a governor to ensure development took place evenly across the northern island. This political change impacted on the colonization policy and the role played by convict labour (Linhart, 1969, p. 56).

The history of forced labour and prisons in Japan

In Japanese as well as European pre-modern times, the dominant social groups used forced labour not only as a means of punishment and producing economic benefits. Being forced to work primarily had the essential function of suppressing unwanted social mobility among the lower classes and forcing those disconnected from social institutions back into their place within the fixed structures (Castel, 2003, p. 50). Historically, the decoupling of relationships from their primary territorial affiliation and the resulting forced mobility constitute a breach of the social contract. In *Capital*, Karl Marx (1990) described the beginnings of the historical movement that produced the modern working class. In this so-called primitive accumulation, the producer is separated from the means of production. Those affected by this two-fold process were on the one hand freed from their feudal servitude, yet on the other hand they lost the subsistence assurance provided by the feudal institution (Marx, 1990, pp. 874–875). As a consequence, masses of people became homeless and unoccupied:

> The proletariat created by the breaking-up of the band of feudal retainers and by the forcible expropriation of the people from the soil, this free and rightless proletariat could not possibly be absorbed into the nascent manufacturers as fast as it was thrown upon the world. On the other hand, these men, suddenly dragged from their accustomed mode of life, could not immediately adapt themselves to the discipline of their new condition. They were turned in massive quantities into beggars, robbers and vagabonds, partly from inclination, in most cases under the force of circumstances.
>
> (Marx, 1990, p. 896)

At roughly the same time as Marx, Pope Leo XIII (1891) also highlighted in his encyclical on capital and labour *Rerum Novarum* the problem of the workers' situation in the face of social changes brought about by industrialization and modernization. The pope, too, viewed with concern the dissolution of feudal economic relationships and the non-existence of protective mechanisms for workers at the start of the industrial age:

> In any case we clearly see, and on this there is general agreement, that some opportune remedy must be found quickly for the misery and

wretchedness pressing so unjustly on the majority of the working class: for the ancient workingmen's guilds were abolished in the last century, and no other protective organization took their place.

(Leo XIII, 1891, #3)

The processes of primitive accumulation took place in many places around the world. Whether in the English workhouses, the Dutch *Rasphuis*, or the Japanese *ninsoku yoseba*, the issue at stake was the following of economic imperatives to forcibly set "useless" vagrant individuals to work, thus suppressing their mobility. It was at the same time that institutional confinement with the aim of transforming people's conduct entered the penal system (Melossi, 2018, pp. 27–40).

This emergence of the modern prison and the role of labour therein has fascinated many scholars and led to seminal works such as Michel Foucault's (1991) *Discipline and Punish*. According to Foucault, the prison resorts to the models of cell, hospital and workshop: the politico-moral model of individual isolation and hierarchy; the technico-medical model of normalization; and the economic model of force applied to compulsory work (Foucault, 1991, p. 248). Work, in this context, is generally monotonous. But, as Foucault emphasizes, it also aims at transforming convicts into workers. This is what Foucault finally identifies as the real economic use of prison work: "producing individuals mechanized according to the general norms of an industrial society" (Foucault, 1991, p. 242). Wages for prison work therefore are not compensation for the yielding of a workforce, but aim instead to give prisoners an understanding of civic values including thrift, property and planning for the future, thus supporting the moral improvement of each individual. Based on these theoretical works of Foucault, a whole range of prison studies have emerged. Indeed, there are numerous studies of the history of the prison in Western countries (Morris and Rothman, 1998; O'Brian, 1982) and in many countries in Asia, Africa and Latin America (Botsman, 2005; Dikötter, 2002; Dikötter and Brown, 2007; Morin and Moran, 2015; Salvatore and Aguirre, 1996; Zinoman, 2001).

Importantly, this growing body of scholarly literature cautions against a dogmatic adoption of a Foucauldian perspective. For example, Salvatore and Aguirre (1996, p. ix) note that "the adaption of Western penal institutions in Latin America was controversial and complex". Contributions in their edited volume *The Birth of the Penitentiary in Latin America* highlight how in spite of reformers' efforts to adapt European and North American ideas of punishment in Latin American countries, the outcomes of these adaptations largely diverged from the original designs. Likewise, Frank Dikötter and Ian Brown's (2007) edited volume *Cultures of Confinement. A History of the Prison in Africa, Asia and Latin America* demonstrates that the theoretical concept and idea of the prison differs from actual global prison practices. In the introduction to the book, Dikötter argues against theories of "cultural imperialism" or "world capitalism" which see Western institutions as having been simply imported and replicated by non-Western countries or colonies. Instead, he emphasizes the fruitfulness of comparative approaches to history that focus on how ideas and concepts are adjusted into local political configurations. Such an approach allows us to discern new varieties of imprisonment: "underneath an overarching rationale based on the idea of humane and reformative punishment, the prison was multivalent, capable of being adopted in a variety of mutually incompatible environments" (Dikötter, 2007, p. 6). In Morin and Moran's (2015) edited collection *Historical Geographies of Prisons*, contributors examine the political-economic setting within and beyond prisons. Case studies in this book challenge the works of theorists who have conceptualized prison as a "total institution" (Goffman, 1991) or a space of discipline (Foucault, 1991). Instead, the authors suggest a considerable porosity of prisons:

> prisons are porous in terms of movements of inmates, staff, goods and services, communications and so on, they are also porous in that their 'transcarceral' nature and techniques pervade the locale, particularly in places which have come to be defined by imprisonment.
> (Morin and Moran, 2015, p. 5)

Research in the English language on Japan indeed highlights how during the Meiji Restoration European ideas of imprisonment were adapted to and transformed the Japanese penal system. These studies emphasize the emergence of institutional structures of arrest and forced labour during the Tokugawa period (Umemori, 2002; Botsman, 2005). The socio-political context at that time was marked by the political persecution of Christians, social unrest related to natural disasters and poverty caused by the economic policies of the Anei period. In the Meiji period, the further development of institutions for incarceration was again part of the political persecution of the religious, political activists and intellectuals (Bowen, 1980; Croydon, 2016, pp. 50–51; Ketelaar, 1990; Mitchell, 1992; Vlastos, 2006). Forced labour was throughout the Tokugawa period an important means of social control and of economic activity at different urban and rural sites (Botsman, 2005; Shigematsu, 2005; Nakagawara, 1988; Umemori, 2002). During the early Meiji period, convict labour was crucial to the industrialization and rural development of Japan (Mason, 2012; Miyamoto, 2017). My research builds on these works as my case study of prison and forced labour during the colonization of Hokkaido similarly challenges dominant Western theories on the "modern prison" as a "total institution".

Turning our focus on Hokkaido's prisons, the 1968 centenary of Hokkaido's development (*kaitaku*) was an important turning point in Hokkaido historiography. Importantly, the official celebrations did not mention prisoners' contribution to the Meiji colonization of Hokkaido at all. As a reaction to this omission, Shigematsu Kazuyoshi published in 1970 his pioneering work *Hokkaido gyōkei shi* (The History of Prison Sentencing in Hokkaido). Local residents also started to form popular movements to shed light on prisoners' hidden contribution to the development of Hokkaido. The movements' history workshops were organized by individuals such as the son of a *tondenhei* family, Nakazawa Hiroshi, the Buddhist nun Hayashi Ryūkō and the social historian Koike (Kikō) Yoshitaka (Oda, 2016, pp. 131–132). The declared aim of these movements was to "unearth" (*horiokosu*) the history of Hokkaido (CDKGTHK, 1993, p. 5). In the early 1970s researchers drew attention to members of the Movement for Freedom and People's Rights (*Jiyū minken undo*) who were sentenced to imprisonment and hard labour in Hokkaido (Koike, 1981; Tomono, 1972). In the second half of the 1980s, we see an increased active engagement with the issue. Nasu Kunie (1987) wrote a study on the eating habits in Sorachi Prison, and in 1988 Nakagawara Takashi's history of prison sentencing in modern Hokkaido was published (Nakagawara, 1988). The 36th Special Exhibition of the Hokkaido Kaitaku Kinenkan (Museum of the Development of Hokkaido) in 1989 was another important event for the research of forced labour. Indeed, the museum's main focus was on the central prisons and the work of prisoners in the course of land development (HKK, 1989). Addressing forced labour had, so to speak, become socially acceptable. From the early 1990s onwards, in time for the approaching centenary of the Chūō road, an important national highway cutting across Hokkaido, a number of publications commemorating the prisoners who died in the course of its construction were published (ASKSKK, 1992; CDKGTHK, 1993). *Hokkaido shūjikan ronkō* (Studies on Hokkaido Prisons), edited by legal historians Takashio Hiroshi and Nakayama Kōshō, was published in 1997; this volume's contributions are mainly presentations of and comments on primary sources (Takashio and Nakayama, 1997). On the whole, my research establishes a historiographic imbalance in secondary literature regarding research on the use of prison labour on Hokkaido. While the phase after 1886 is relatively well documented, comparatively little is written about the first 5 years of prisons on Hokkaido. One possible reason for this imbalance may be that a transformation of forced labour started in 1886. The majority of casualties suffered by convicts resulted from their use as forced labour in mining and road construction, which may explain why the period after 1886 received so much attention during the commemorations. This focus, however, has also led to a distorted image of the relationship between the prisons and the local population. Due to the number of attempted escapes while working outside the prison in the period after 1886, the population of Hokkaido felt increasingly troubled and threatened by working prisoners. Yet, before 1886, we can observe a completely different relationship where prisons fulfilled important social functions in their region, with prisoners working, amongst others, as craftsmen for private individuals.

Book structure

After this introduction, the main body of the study follows in four parts. Chapter 1 examines forced labour and arrest in early modern Japan, focusing on Ezo and Matsumae *han* (Hokkaido) as a space of arrest and forced labour. Chapter 2 explains how after the Meiji Restoration (1868) politicians conceptualized Hokkaido as a prison island first for political convicts, then also for non-political criminals. Chapters 3 and 4 document the deployment of convict labour on Hokkaido. Data presented in these chapters suggest a coincidence between colonial policy and the mobilization of prison labour between the years 1881 and 1894. In particular, Chapter 3 outlines prisoners' contributions to processes of rural development through farming and industrial activities. The chapter also draws attention to the sociopolitical role prisons played in their surrounding communities. Chapter 4 shifts the attention to the transformation of Japans' prison labour policy from 1886 onwards. As a consequence of this policy change, forced labour in Hokkaido's prisons focused between 1886 and 1894 on road construction and the extraction of coal and sulphur. The conclusion summarizes and discusses the contributions of Japan's forced prison labour project on its first colony, Hokkaido.

Source material

The primary sources used in this study can be divided into three groups: firstly, prison reports and the statistics contained therein; secondly, letters by the authorities; and thirdly, contemporary witness statements.

The first principal source for this study are three prison reports which were collectively published under the title *Shūjikan (kangokusho) shiryō* (Historical Sources on the Central Institutions [Prisons]) by the City of Asahikawa. The first report is described as *Shūjikan enkaku chō* (Report on the History of Prisons) and was compiled in 1894 for the 2nd Imperial Parliament session, where it was intended for use as illustrative material for cost estimate negotiations. The reports on each individual prison, however, were sent to the Hokkaido-chō in such an uncoordinated fashion that it is highly doubtful they were actually used in the context of the parliamentary session.

The second report, *Kabato shūjikan enkaku ryakki* (Brief Account of the History of the Kabato Prison), consists of two parts. The first part has the same title as the report and was initially published in 1885; it was later reworked to such an extent that it included information up to 1887. As the title of the report indicates, it is a short account of the Kabato Prison. The second part, *Hokkaido shūjikan yōran* (Overview of the History of Hokkaido Prisons), was written in 1892, after Kabato had been restructured into the main institution and the other prisons into branch institutions. The two reports were later combined at an unknown date (Hirano, 1992, p. 339).

The third report is a chronology of the events at Sorachi Prison. This independent publication had been planned before the *Shūjikan enkaku chō* was compiled and was finished in November 1891. Unlike the other reports, the *Sorachi bunkan enkaku ku* (Writings on the History of the Branch Institution of Sorachi) reproduces letters from individuals. The originals of the three reports are unfortunately no longer in existence; they were transferred to the present Asahikawa Prison after the closing of the main institution of Kabato in 1919 and then moved to the Ministry of Justice in 1938 but were subsequently destroyed during the Second World War (Hirano, 1992, p. 339). Bibliographer Hirano Tomohiko does not disclose any information about the authors of these three reports, and the source text is equally lacking. We may therefore assume that their authors were anonymous prison secretaries.

The second principal source for this study are letters from Japanese authorities. For the most part, these letters have been reprinted in Shigematsu's, 1970 book and in the Asahikwa collection of source material in their original style in the collection edited by Takeshio and Nakayama. Like the prison reports, these texts were not originally meant for public inspection.

The third group of primary materials are statements by contemporary witnesses, all non-state actors. Important among them are the 18th-century report of Fray Diego de San Francisco's captivity in Edo (Martinez, 1756), as well as the 19th-century memoirs of the Russian Captain Golownin (1824a, b) who with his crew was held captive in Ezo during the years 1811–1813. Another important source is the record of an oral report by a former prison guard named Maruta Yoshio. With some former colleagues, Maruta took part in a round table discussion on the Kushiro Prison at the primary school in Shibecha on 7 July 1940, organized by the *Kushiro jitoku kai* (Kushiro Society for Love and Virtue). One striking feature of this source is its date, which bears witness to an early local historical interest in the contributions of the forced labourers of Kushiro Prison. In addition, the discussions recorded reveal a prisoner-friendly context which suggests a very humane and compassionate reporting of the events of the past. Whether the attitudes of the guards reflect their attitudes at the time of events is not known. It is therefore essential to understand these testimonies as (re)constructions of the past. Parts of these discussion records have been quoted repeatedly in secondary literature, but the complete version is printed only in Takashio and Nakayama's (1997) book.

To better understand the historical development of penal servitude in Japan, the next chapter turns to imprisonment and forced labour in early modern Japan with a geographical focus on Ezo (Hokkaido).

Bibliography

Amino, Y. 1992, Deconstructing "Japan". *East Asian History*, 3, pp. 121–142.

Amino, Y. 2000, *"Nihon" to ha nani ka*. Tokyo: Kodansha.

Anaya, S.J. 1996, *Indigenous People in International Law*. New York and Oxford: Oxford University Press.

Anderson, M. 2010, *A Place in Public: Women's Rights in Meiji Japan*. Cambridge and London: Harvard University Press.

ASKSKK = Abashiri shichō kannai sō gō kaihatsu kiseikai. ed. 1992, *Ohōtsuku he no michi. Chūō dō ro hyakunen kinen*. Tōkyō and Sapporo: Abashiri shichō kaihatsu kiseikai.

Beasley, W.G. 1987, *Japanese Imperialism 1894–1945*. Oxford: Clarendon Press.

Botsman, D.V. 2005, *Punishment and Power in the Making of Modern Japan*. Princeton and Oxford: Princeton University Press.

Bowen, R.W. 1980, *Rebellion and Democracy in Meiji Japan: A Study of Commoners in the Popular Rights Movement*. Berkeley, Los Angeles and London: University of California Press.

Burkman, T.W. 1974, The Urakami Incidents and the Struggle for Religious Toleration in Early Meiji Japan. *Japanese Journal of Religious Studies*, 1(2/3), pp. 143–216.

Calman, D. 1992, *The Nature and Origins of Japanese Imperialism*. London and New York: Routledge.

Castel, R. 2003, *From Manual Workers to Wage Laborers: Transformation of the Social Question*. New Brunswick and London: Transaction Publishers.

CDKGTHK = Chūō dōro giseisha tsuitō hikensetsu kiseikai, ed. 1993, *Rupeshipe no bohyō: Chūō dōro ni taoreta torawarebito e no chinkonfu*. Rubeshibe: Chūō dōro giseisha tsuitō hikensetsu kiseikai.

Christy, A.S. 1997, The Making of Imperial Subjects in Okinawa. In Barlow, T.E. ed. *Formations of Colonial Modernity in East Asia*. Durham and London: Duke University Press, pp. 141–167.

Croydon, S. 2016, *The Politics of Police Detention in Japan: Consensus of Convenience*. Oxford: Oxford University Press.

Dikötter, F. 2002, *Crime, Punishment and the Prison in Modern China*. London: Hurst.

Dikötter, F. 2007, Introduction. In Dikötter, F. and Brown, I. eds. *Cultures of Confinement: A History of the Prison in Africa, Asia and Latin America*. London: Hurst, pp. 1–13.

14 *Introduction*

Dikötter, F. and Brown, I. eds. 2007, *Cultures of Confinement: A History of the Prison in Africa, Asia and Latin America*. London: Hurst.

Enomoto, M. 1999, *Hokkaido no rekishi*. Sapporo: Hokkaido shinbunsha.

Foucault, M. 1991, *Discipline and Punishment: The Birth of the Prison*. London: Penguin Books.

Goffman, E. 1991, *Asylums: Essays on the Social Situation of Mental Patients and Other Inmates*. London: Penguin Books.

Golownin, V.M. 1824a, *Memoirs of a Captivity in Japan, During the Years 1811, 1812, and 1813: With Observations on the Country and People. Vol. 1*. London: Henry Colburn & Co.

Golownin, V.M. 1824b, *Memoirs of a Captivity in Japan, During the Years 1811, 1812, and 1813: With Observations on the Country and People. Vol. 2*. London: Henry Colburn & Co.

Hirano, K. 2017, Settler Colonialism in the making of Japan's Hokkaidō. In Cavanagh, E. and Veracini, L. eds. *The Routledge Handbook of the History of Settler Colonialism*. London: Routledge, pp. 268–277.

Hirano, T. 1992, Kaidai. In ASKSKK = Abashiri shichō kannai sō gō kaihatsu kiseikai. ed. *Ohōtsuku e no michi: Chūō dō ro hyakunen kinen*. Tokyo and Sapporo: Abashiri shichō kaihatsu kiseikai, pp. 337–340.

HKK = Hokkaido kaitaku kinenkan, ed. 1989, *Shūjikan. Kaitaku to shūjinrō dō*. Sapporo: Hokkaido kaitaku kinenkan.

Howell, D.L. 2005, *Geographies of Identity in Nineteenth-Century Japan*. Berkeley: University of California Press.

Hudson, M.J. 2014, Ainu and Hunter-Gatherer Studies. In Hudson, M.J., lewallen, a.-e. and Watson, M.K. eds. *Beyond Ainu Studies: Changing Academic and Public Perspectives*. Honolulu: University of Hawaii Press, pp. 117–135.

Huffman, J.L. 2006, Restoration and Revolution. In Tutsui, W.M. ed. *A Companion to Japanese History*. Blackwell Reference Online. www.blackwellreference.com/subscriber/tocnode.html?id=g9781405116909_chunk_g978140511690911, accessed 14 March 2018.

Irish, A.B. 2009, *Hokkaido: A History of Ethnic Transition and Development on Japan's Northern Island*. Jefferson, NC and London: McFarland and Company.

Ketelaar, J.E. 1990, *Of Heretics and Martyrs in Meiji Japan. Buddhism and Its Persecution*. Princeton: Princeton University Press.

Koike, Y. 1981 [¹1973], *Kusaritsuka: Jiyūminken to shūjin rōdō no kiroku*. Tokyo: Gendaishi shuppankai.

Komori, Y. 2001, *Posutokoroniaru*. Tokyo: Iwanami shoten.

Komori, Y. 2012, Rule in the Name of "Protection": The Vocabulary of Colonialism. In Mason M.M. and Lee, H. eds. *Reading Colonial Japan: Text, Context, and Critique*. Redwood City: Stanford University Press, pp. 60–75.

Konishi, S. 2007, Reopening the "Opening of Japan": A Russian-Japanese Revolutionary Encounter and the Vision of Anarchist Progress. *American Historical Review*, 112(1), pp. 101–130.

Kreiner, J. and Ölschleger, H-D. eds. 1987, *Ainu. Jäger, Fischer und Sammler im Norden Japans*. Köln: Rautenstrauch-Joest-Museum der Stadt Köln.

Leo XIII. 1891, *Rerum Novarum: Encyclical of Pope Leo XIII on Capital and Labor*. Vatican: Libreria Editrice Vaticana.

lewallen, a-e. 2016a, *The Fabric of Indigeneity: Ainu Identity, Gender, and Settler Colonialism in Japan*. Santa Fe and Albuquerque: School of Advanced Research Press and University of New Mexico Press.

Lewallen, a-e. 2016b, 'Clamoring Blood': The Materiality of Belonging in Modern Ainu Identity. *Critical Asian Studies*, 48/1, 50–76.

Linhart, S. 1969, The Frontier Spirit of Hokkaido: Illusion and Reality. In Slawik, A. and Kreiner, J. eds. *Beiträge zur Japanologie. Vol. 6*. Vienna: Institute of Japanese Studies, pp. 53–71.

Martinez, D. 1756, *Compendio Histórico de la Apostolica Provincia de San Gregorio de Philipinas, de Religiosos descalzos de N.P. San Francisco*. Madrid: En la Imprenta de la Viuda de Manuel Fernandez y del Supremo Consejo de la Inquisicion.

Marx, K. 1990, *Capital. A Critique of Political Economy. Vol. 1*. London: Penguin Books.

Mason, M. 2012, *Dominant Narratives of Colonial Hokkaido and Imperial Japan*. London: Palgrave Macmillan.

Matsusaka, Y.T. 2006, The Japanese Empire. In Tsutsui, W.M. ed. *A Companion to Japanese History*. Blackwell Reference Online. www.blackwellreference.com/subscriber/tocnode.html?id=g9781405116909_chunk_g978140511690916, accessed 14 March 2018.

Melossi, D. 2018, Creation of the Modern Prison in England and Europe (1550–1850). In Melossi, D. and Pavarini, M. eds. *The Prison and the Factory (40th Anniversary Edition): Origins of the Penitentiary System*. London: Palgrave Macmillan, pp. 27–95.

Mitchell, R.H. 1992, *Janus-Faced Justice: Political Crimes in Imperial Japan*. Honolulu: University of Hawaii Press.

Miyamoto, T. 2017, Convict Labor and Its Commemoration: The Mitsui Miike Coal Mine Experience. *The Asia-Pacific Journal*, 15/1, pp. 1–15.

Morin, K.M. and Moran, D. 2015, Introduction: Historical Geographies of Prisons: Unlocking the Usable Carceral Past. In Morin, K.M. and Moran, D. eds. *Historical Geographies of Prisons: Unlocking the Usable Carceral Past*. Abingdon and New York: Routledge, pp. 1–13.

Morris, N. and Rothman, D.J. eds. 1998, *The Oxford History of the Prison: The Practice of Punishment in Western Society*. New York and Oxford: Oxford University Press.

Morris-Suzuki, T. 1994, Creating the Frontier: Border, Identity and History in Japan's Far North. *East Asian History*, 7, pp. 1–24.

Morris-Suzuki, T. 1995, Sustainability and Ecological Colonialism in Edo Period Japan. *Japanese Studies*, 15/1, pp. 36–48.

Morris-Suzuki, T. 2013, Letters to the Dead: Grassroots Historical Dialogue in East Asia's Borderlands. In Morris-Suzuki, T. et al. eds. *East Asia Beyond the History Wars: Confronting the Ghosts of Violence*. London: Routledge, pp. 87–104.

Nagai, M. and Urrutia, M. eds. 1985, *Meiji Ishin. Restauration and Revolution*. Tokyo: United Nations University.

16   *Introduction*

Nakagawara, T. 1988, *Kinsei Hokkaido gyō keishi*. Tokyo: Dōsei.
Nasu, K. 1987, *Sorachi shūjikan no shokuseikatsu*. Iwamizawa: Hokkaido shinbunsha.
O'Brian, P. 1982, *The Promise of Punishment: Prisons in Nineteenth-Century France*. Princeton: Princeton University Press.
Oda, H. 2016, Unearthing the History of *minshū* in Hokkaido: The case study of the Okhotsk People's History Workshop. In Seaton, P. ed. *Local History and War Memories in Hokkaido*. London: Routledge, pp. 129–158.
Oguma, E. 2017, *The Boundaries of 'the Japanese': Vol. 2. Korea, Taiwan and the Ainu 1868–1945*. Melbourne: Trans Pacific Press.
Peattie, M. 2008, The Japanese Colonial Empire, 1895–1945. In Duus, P. ed. *The Cambridge History of Japan, Vol. 6: The Twentieth Century*. Cambridge: Cambridge University Press, pp. 217–270.
Salvatore, R.D. and Aguirre, C. 1996, Introduction. In Salvatore, R.D. and Aguirre, C. eds. *The Birth of the Penitentiary in Latin America: Essays on Criminology, Prison Reform, and Social Control, 1830–1940*. Austin: University of Texas Press, pp. ix–xxi.
Scheiner, I. 1970, *Christian Converts and Social Protest in Meiji Japan*. Berkeley and Los Angeles: University of California Press.
Seaton, P. 2016, Grand Narratives of Empire and Development. In Seaton, P. ed. *Local History and War Memories in Hokkaido*. London: Routledge, pp. 26–59.
Seaton, P. 2017, Japanese Empire in Hokkaido. In *Oxford Research Encyclopedia of Asian History*. http://ezproxy-prd.bodleian.ox.ac.uk:4362/view/10.1093/acrefore/9780190277727.001.0001/acrefore-9780190277727-e-76, accessed 14 March 2018.
Shigematsu, K. 1970, *Hokkaido gyō keishi*. Tokyo: Zufu shuppan.
Shigematsu, K. 2005, *Nihon gokuseishi no kenkyū*. Tokyo: Yoshikawa Kōbunkan.
Siddle, R. 1996, *Race, Resistance and the Ainu of Japan*. London and New York: Routledge.
Siddle, R. 1997, The Ainu and the Discourse of 'Race'. In Dikötter, F. ed. *The Construction of Racial Identities in China and Japan: Historical and Contemporary Perspectives*. London: Hurst, pp. 136–157.
Steger, B. 1994, From Impurity to Hygiene: The Role of Midwives in the Modernisation of Japan. *Japan Forum*, 6(2), 175–178.
Takashio, H. and Nakayama, K. eds. 1997, *Hokkaido shūjikan ronkō*. Tokyo: Kōbundō.
Tomono, S. 1972, *Gokusō no jiyū minkenshatachi: Hokkaidō shūchikan no secchi*. Sapporo: Miyami Sōsho.
Umemori, N. 2002, *Modernization Through Colonial Mediations: The Establishment of the Police and Prison System in Meiji Japan* (Order No. 3070223). Available from ProQuest Dissertations & Theses Global. (305505033). https://ezproxy-prd.bodleian.ox.ac.uk:7316/docview/305505033?accountid=13042, accessed 15 March 2018.
Vlastos, S. 2006, Opposition Movements in Early Meiji, 1868–1885. In Jansen, M.B. ed. *The Cambridge History of Japan: Vol. 5*. Cambridge: Cambridge University Press, pp. 367–431.

Walker, B.L. 2001, *The Conquest of Ainu Lands: Ecology and Culture in Japanese Expansion, 1590–1800*. Berkeley and London: University of California Press.

Walthall, A. 1998, *The Weak Body of a Useless Woman: Matsuo Taseko and the Meiji Restauration*. Chicago and London: The University of Chicago Press.

Wigen, K. 1995, *The Making of a Japanese Periphery, 1750–1920*. Berkeley: University of California Press.

Zinoman, P. 2001, *The Colonial Bastille: A History of Imprisonment in Vietnam, 1862–1940*. Oxford: Oxford University Press.

1 Forced labour and arrest in Edo and Ezo

From the Kamakura period (1185–1333) onwards, Ezo has been a place of exile. For instance, in 1191, thieves were sent to Ezo, and from 1216 pirates were sent there, too. Importantly, the legal code of the Kamakura shogunate, the *Goseibai Shikimoku* (Formulary of Adjudications), promulgated in 1232, mentioned "exile to Ezo" (*Ezo shima rukei*) as punishment (Nakagawara, 1988, p. 3). During the early Tokugawa period, there was an initial lack of cooperation between Matsumae *han* and Edo (Hall, 1955, p. 101) which impacted on Ezo as a space of exile and banishment. For example, after the promulgation of Tokugawa Ieyasu's anti-Christian edict in 1614, Christians were exiled to northern Japan. Some found refuge in Ezo where it was still possible to practice their faith (Cieslik, 1941, p. 320; Shigematsu, 2011, p. 148). As a consequence, priests travelled in disguise to these northern territories to visit the exiled Christian communities. When the Jesuit Girolamo de Angelis arrived in 1619, he was – in spite of his disguise – recognized as a priest. However, the daimyo of Matsumae reportedly told de Angelis that he had nothing to fear because "Matsuame is not Japan" (Boxer, 1993, p. 344).

Yet, similar to other *han*, Matsumae *han* also had a system of forced labour camps (*ninsoku yoseba*) and arrest houses (*rōya*). These institutions were antecedents to the Meiji Prison where forced labour and imprisonment turned into the principal form of punishment.

The *ninsoku yoseba* in Edo

The first forms of institutionalized forced labour emerged as a Tokugawa policy response to the rising number of dispossessed and homeless people in the 1770s and 1780s. During these years, natural disaster and crop failure caused the general population's living conditions to worsen. In many rural areas, farmers were forced to abandon their fields. At the same time, the number of peasant uprisings increased, and in the cities the anger of starving citizens turned into attacks on the residences of moneylenders and the warehouses of wholesale merchants (*uchi kowashi*). In the year 1786 Japan's entire agricultural production was cut by two-thirds. Yet, the *bakufu* was unwilling and unable to alleviate the populace's distress (Hall, 1955, pp. 122–127). Eventually, the government's Kansei Reforms (1789–1801) aimed at the re-establishment of public safety, including coping with rising numbers of dispossessed and homeless people (Botsman, 1999, p. 203). Thus, in 1789, Hasegawa Heizō, the *bakufu* official in charge of all cases of arson and theft, drafted plans for an enclosed work camp (*ninsoku yoseba*) on Ishikawajima, an island at the mouth of the Sumida River in Edo. The declared goal of this *ninsoku yoseba* was the re-education of marginalized individuals into farmers and shop owners, by putting inmates' existing skills to work in the camp. Thus, the early labour camps of the Tokugawa period had the declared intention of conditioning their inmates to the wage system through monotonous work processes. Hasegawa introduced economically profitable labour operations, signing contracts with private persons to whom inmates were assigned to serve. In the beginning, tasks focused on the maintenance of the prison facility; however, over time, products for sale on the open market were also produced. Work tasks were divided into three areas: labour, crafting and farming. Labour included tasks such as construction and maintenance of storage facilities, polishing rice for consumption by the *rōya* and the digging of ditches. Inmates were also put to work privately as labourers and bricklayers and were ordered to do repairs in the houses of wealthy families. In crafting, the inmates were occupied in working with straw, processing coal and various woodworking tasks. The forced labourers were likewise hired by private companies to do similar tasks, as well as to transport coal and wood. Warehouse craftsman cut reeds and manufactured reed screens. Although apparently none of the above tasks drew the attention of the wider population of Edo, the recycling of paper in the *yoseba* became very controversial. Nevertheless, enough people supported the paper production so that it remained an important source of income for the facility, along with coal and woodworking, until the closing of the *yoseba*. The agricultural activities of the inmates on Ishikawajima were limited to the reclamation of arable land in the surrounding private estates, and farming to supply the institution (Hiramatsu, 1994, pp. 196–198; Tsukada 1995, p. 34). Measures were additionally enacted by the government to permit not just vagrants to be sent to the labour camps, but also disobedient servants and juvenile delinquents (Botsman, 1999, pp. 193–194). The year 1820 marked a further turning point in the *ninsoku yoseba*, when camp regulations were changed so that persons punished with banishment could also be deported to Ishikawajima (Hiramatsu, 1994, p. 206). Thus, the labour camp was used as a penal institution well into the era of the Great Tenpō Famine (1834–1837). However, during this great famine and the increasing vagrancy of the poorest of the poor that came with it, the population of the *yoseba* grew from its usual 150 inmates to around 400. So, to address the prison's limited capacity in 1838 the admission of banished persons was halted and once again only homeless people were admitted. In Tenpō 12 (1841), after the situation in the region had calmed and the number of inmates had subsided, banishment sentences were once again replaced by deportation to the *yoseba* (Tsukada, 1995, p. 36).

In 1842, the arrest of vagrants arose again as the result of Chancellor Mizuno Tadakuni's order to relocate all homeless and beggars to their village of origin. The majority of these marginalized individuals were, however, from Edo and its surroundings and so could not be sent back to countryside areas. These people were instead detained in Ishikawajima, with the camp reaching its highest population, 600 inmates, in 1844 as a direct result of this political measure.

Mizuno also ordered the establishment of a *ninsoku yoseba* network in areas under the direct control of the *bakufu* as well as in each *han* (Botsman, 1999, pp. 219–220). Following this order, the construction of four *ninsoku yoseba* in Osaka, Kyoto, Akita and Hakodate started in 1860 (Shigematsu, 2005, p. 167). The next section thus turns to focusing on the *ninsoku yoseba* in Ezo's Matsumae *han*.

The *ninsoku yoseba* in Ezo

The plans to establish the first *ninsoku yoseba* in Hakodate were intimately related to the *bakufu's* economic and political concerns. In the Treaty of Kanagawa (1854), Commodore Perry asked for the opening of the ports of Shimoda and Hakodate. Furthermore, after the signing of the Treaty of Shimoda (1855), the Kuril islands were divided between the Russian Empire and Tokugawa Japan. Thus, the opening of the port of Hakodate and the geographical closeness of the Russian Empire emphasized Japanese ideas of Hakodate being "the lock of the northern gate" (*kiitamon sayaku*), and urgently called for the "development of Ezo" (*Ezochi kaitaku*) (Shigematsu, 2005, p. 168). In this context, the establishment of a *ninsoku yoseba* in Hakodate seemed like a good plan as vagrants and criminals could be used as a cheap labour force for local development plans. However, the initial plan of a *yoseba* in Hakodate was dropped due to a scarcity of land and also because of concerns about potential moral decay. Proposals for alternative places included Daikoku Island and Okushiri Island, located off the shores of Eastern and Western Ezo, respectively. Eventually, the work camp was established in Usubetsu with a branch on Okushiri Island. Thus, the camp was referred to as *Usubetsu Okushirishima ninsoku yoseba* (Shigematsu, 2005, p. 168). Usubetsu served for a long time as a place of exile in the Matsumae *han*. Because of the construction of the *yoseba*, the infrastructure in the areas around Usubetsu improved and it eventually became a work camp that specialized in fishing industries (Shigematsu, 2005, p. 169). In 1860, another *yoseba* was constructed in Shiranuka located in Western Ezo. Most of the inmates there were criminals sent to work in the mines (Enomoto, 1999, p. 159). In 1861 a branch office of the *bugyo* (magistrate) of Hakodate was set up on Okushiri Island; this island, too, was used a space of exile for criminal offenders with light sentences. They worked in fishery specializing in produce such as sea urchins, sea snails, mackerel and wakame (Shigematsu, 2011, p. 149).

The institution of the *ninsoku yoseba* thus added another dimension to different forms of forced labour – such as the exploitation of Ainu labour in the *basho* system explained earlier – in early modern Ezo. The next section turns to early modern forms of imprisonment in Ezo.

Arrest in Edo

In early modern Japan, imprisonment was usually not a punishment in itself. Instead, the main function of arrest houses (*rōya*) was the detainment of suspects and as a holding space for those sentenced as guilty and awaiting their punishment. The *rōya* also served as a location for the execution of punishments such as decapitation, flogging and tattooing. Although it was used for people serving penalties of life imprisonment and imprisonments of a short period of 30 days, life imprisonment was specially reserved for persons charged with the death penalty or with exile to an island but who for some reason had received special consideration from the authorities (Hiramatsu, 1994, pp. 174–175).

The first *rōya* was founded under Toyotomi Hideyoshi's rule about 10 years before the 1603 establishment of the Tokugawa shogunate. Between 1596 and 1615 this arrest house moved to the Kodenmachō quarter of Edo near Nihonbashi, where it operated until the early Meiji period (Botsman, 1992, p. 9). The *rōya* in Edo's Kodenmachō was possibly the largest institution of its kind and could hold up to 700 inmates, although the number of inmates was usually between 300 and 400. The *rōya* accommodated its inmates according to their social status and gender. Relatively luxurious accommodations were reserved for direct vassals of the Shogun, and lower vassals, doctors and priests were also given relatively comfortable *agariya.* These rooms were well lit and usually had a place to wash, a latrine and tatami flooring. Commoners were held in a general prison, farmers in a separate prison and women in a general women's prison regardless of their social status (Nakagawara, 1988, p. 168). This confinement of women was, during the early Tokugawa period, a way to punish by association the female relatives of male criminals. By the late Tokugawa period, women who were themselves petty offenders were also gradually sentenced to short periods of arrest. This replaced the *bakufu*'s previous practice of punishing petty crimes by severing men and women's ears and nose (Botsman, 2014, pp. 139–140).

Speaking was permitted in prisons except during the night time curfew. Smoking pipes was very common, even if it was officially forbidden to consume tobacco. Except for an occasional visit to the *bugyō* (commissioner), inmates generally did not leave their cells. In Edo during this period, they were usually not made to work and passed the time by playing Go, *shōgi* and various games of chance (Hiramatsu, 1994, pp. 175–176).

The *rōya* was different, however, in other parts of Edo and elsewhere in Japan. For example, a detailed account exists of the Spanish missionary Fray Diego de San Francisco's 18-months imprisonment in a jail in Edo. This account was given in Fray Domingo Martinez's (1761) *Compendio Historico de la Apostolica Provincia de San Gregorio de Philipinas.* He was captured on 14 April 1615 together with two Japanese companions. After being interrogated, they were sent to the public prison in Edo. This prison consisted of a square wooden building. The prisoners were kept in a cage inside this building. The cage measured roughly 10 metres (12 *varas*) by 4.18 metres (5 *varas*), and its wooden bars were so wide that almost no daylight could enter and prisoners spent their days in darkness. The cage had no windows, except for a little opening through which food and water was passed. Usually there were between 100 and 153 prisoners. They had to take off their clothes before entering the cage and were only allowed to wear a cloth to cover their private parts. No objects were allowed. Due to the narrow space, prisoners had to sit huddled on the floor in three rows so that it was impossible to stretch their legs without touching the other prisoners. It is unsurprising there was a lot of tension among the prisoners and records show they often hit and hurt each other. Worms and lice infestations were commonplace. Up to 30–40 prisoners could be ill at any one time, relieving themselves wherever they had been put. They were thus left lying in their own excrements and the jail stank. Prisoners were generally undernourished as the small amounts of rice they were given was insufficient to sustain an adult person. There was never enough rice provided for everyone so some of the prisoners starved to death, especially the sick who were unable to move and were often deprived of their portion. There was also a severe shortage of water. Each prisoner received one small cup of water in the morning and another in the late afternoon. Severe dehydration was widespread (Martinez, 1756, pp. 167–171).

Arrest in Ezo

The *rōya* in Matsumae *han* differed considerably from the *rō* in Edo's Kodenmachō, as well as from the general prison in which Fray Diego de San Francisco was kept for 18 months. An important source for the arrest house conditions in Matsumae-*han* is the testimony of the Russian Captain Vasily M Golownin. In 1811, Golownin and his crew reached the shore of Kunashir, the southernmost part of the Kurile Islands. The *bakufu* considered this area, which is part of Ezo-chi, as territory belonging to Japan (Oguma, 2017, pp. 16–17). So, by entering Kunashir, Golownin and his six companions had transgressed Japan's seclusion policy (*sakoku*) (Hall, 2008, p. 5). This policy only allowed Dutch and Chinese ships to enter Japanese territory through Dejima in Nagasaki. Golownin and his companions spent two years in total as prisoners of the Japanese in Ezo. After his return to St Petersburg, Golownin described his time of captivity in Ezo. His account was translated into several languages, including English with the title, *Japan and the Japanese: Comprising the Narrative of a Captivity in Japan* (Golownin, 1824a, b). In his memoirs, Golownin provides a detailed account of the various arrest houses he and his companions were kept in. They were initially placed in a prison in Hakodate. Golownin notes that their first sight of the prison "filled us with horror". The long and dark wooden building looked like a barn and was surrounded by a strong wooden fence and a *cheval-de-frise* (i.e. a portable frame covered with projecting long iron or wooden spikes or spears). Inside, the building was structured in "apartments formed of strong thick spars of wood, which, but for the differences of size, looked exactly like bird-cages" (Golownin, 1824a, p. 126). The Japanese guards insisted the sailors remained in the presence of one of their own Russian officers "who would teach them, by his example and advice, to bear unavoidable misfortunes; adding that the men might otherwise lose courage, and become the victims of despair" (Golownin, 1824a, p. 127). In contrast to the *rōya* in Kondemachō, this arrest house in Hakodate did not group prisoners according to their social status, the guards appeared to take into consideration the psychological needs of the lower ranking men (i.e. the sailors), believing they would be encouraged by the example of the higher ranking men (i.e. the officers). To his dismay, however, Captain Golownin was separated from his companions and locked up alone. In his memoirs he frankly expresses the despair he felt at this moment. The entire group was later transferred to a prison in Matsumae which Golownin describes vividly:

> It was a quadrangular wooden building, twenty-five paces long, fifteen broad, and twelve feet high. Three sides were complete wall, without any aperture whatever. (. . .) In the middle were two cages, formed of spars. (. . .) One cage was six paces square, and ten feet high; the other was of an equal breadth and height, but was eight paces long. We three officers were put into the former; the sailors and Alexei were confined in the latter. The entrance of the cage was so low, what we were obliged to creep into it. The door was formed of massy spars, and was fastened by a strong iron bolt. Above the door was a small hole, through which food was handed to us. A small water-closet was constructed at the further end of each cage. The sides of the cage next each other were bounded in such a manner that we could see the sailors, but they could not perceive us; a screen was also placed between the closets, for the purpose of obstructing the view from the one to the other. A guard-room was placed against the spars which formed the entrance side of the prison, and which was occupied by two soldiers in the service of the imperial government, who ware constantly on guard: they could see us and seldom turned their eyes away from us.
>
> (Golownin, 1824a, pp. 192–193)

This prison Golownin describes so meticulously contained features usually associated with "the modern prison": it followed the principle of surveil-lance where guards are able to observe inmates at all times, while simulta-neously employing architectonical devices ("a screen was placed between the closets") to prevent inmates from seeing one another. The prison was located in close proximity to the *bugyo*'s office and Golownin's crew met the *bugyo* on a daily basis to be interviewed. Once the *bugyo* had decided he was personally convinced of their innocence, he upgraded their treat-ment. For example, Golownin describes at length the improved quality of their food. Their menu typically included stewed rice and pickled radishes, boiled or fried fish as well as soups with different herbs and macaroni. Occa-sionally the Russian captives were treated with Russian-style food, such as a "kind of Russian soup or sauce, made with white fish and muscle broth" (Golownin, 1824a, p. 206). Meals were usually given three times a day together with drinks such as lukewarm or hot tea. Their diet changed with seasonal changes. With the beginning of snowfall, for instance, the captives were given the meat of bears and horses. During winter, authorities also adjusted the architecture to better protect the captives from the cold outside (Golownin, 1824a, pp. 206–207). Clothes were another remarkable issue for Captain Golownin who tells how the Japanese authorities made efforts to clothe the Russian captives well enough to survive the cold climate of Ezo. Indeed, shortly after their arrival in the prison a tailor appeared to take their measurements; he also asked whether they preferred to have clothes in Russian or Japanese style (Golownin, 1824a, p. 205).

Golownin emphasizes the contrast between the attention and care – food, furniture, clothes – with the "rigorous confinement" of the cages in which he and his crew were being held (Golownin, 1824a, p. 192). He explains that their arrest house in Matsumae was referred to as an *okiso*. He remarks that this kind of arrest house differed from other arrest houses which were referred to as *ro*.[1] According to his Japanese informants, the main difference between the *okiso* and the *ro* was there was no fire in a *ro*. Also, the inmates of a *ro* were not allowed to consume tea, tobacco or *sagi*.[2] Moreover, the food in a *ro* was reportedly of less quality and rice was only given in limited quantities. Yet, the prison's structure and the practice of strict surveillance were the same for both types of institutions. Initially, Golownin thought that only foreigners were kept in *okiso*; however, when told that Japanese people were also held captive in this kind of institution, he concluded that the *okiso* may be regarded "as a prison of a superior kind" (Golownin, 1824a, pp. 245–266).

During their arrest in Matsumae, Captain Golownin and his companions were also asked to draw maps and work as translators: "The Japanese kept us constantly employed in translating, with the view of making themselves acquainted with the Russian language, but still more out of curiosity and distrust" (Golownin, 1824a, p. 259). Work and confinement were thus not mutually exclusive in all arrest houses throughout early modern Japan.

When Golownin and his companions attempted an escape, they were recaptured and led back to their prison. In his memoirs, he describes their recapture without anger or resentment. Instead, the Russian captain emphasizes the kindness of the Japanese people "whom enlightened Europe has regarded as barbarians":

> When we passed through villages, the inhabitants flocked from all sides to look at us: but to the honour of the Japanese it ought to be observed, that not one of them treated us with anything like derision or mockery; they all seemed to commiserate us, and some of the women even shed tears whilst they presented us with something to eat or drink. Such was the expression of feeling among a people whom enlightened Europe has regarded as barbarians.
>
> (Golownin, 1824b, pp. 40–41)

Eventually, they were put into another prison in Matsumae that resembled the *rōya* in Hakodate described earlier. However, the way they were treated changed drastically: before their escape attempt, they were treated as captives and foreign guests, but afterwards they were treated in the same way as Japanese criminals. Importantly, however, Golownin notes: "We, indeed, through this treatment extremely severe; yet, it must nevertheless be acknowledged, that the Japanese laws respecting criminals are far more human than those of most, I might perhaps say of all, European nations" (Golownin, 1824b, pp. 58–59). He also describes the cleanliness of the arrest house. During their daily visits to the local authorities, the prisoners' cages were cleaned and their coverlets and night-clothes aired in the sunlight. They received meals three times a day, usually consisting of thick boiled rice, soup with seaweed, sweet cabbage and other vegetables. Occasionally they were given two pieces of salt-fish. They drank water and were able to call for as much water as needed even during the night. Golownin emphasizes that "to the honour of the Japanese, I must declare, that many of them treated us with great kindness, and did all they could to afford us consolation" (Golownin, 1824b, p. 60) He gives examples of people who showed them particular kindness. Three guards brought them refreshments and replaced their vessels with water and with tea. Another soldier who was on duty during the night of their escape "presented the most striking example of humanity" (Golownin, 1824b, p. 61). Because his neglect allowed the Russians to escape, the soldier was downgraded to a common servant and accompanied the group searching for the escapees. After the Russians were recaptured, this man

> saluted us kindly the first moment he beheld us; and far from testifying the least hatred or ill-will, made every exertion to serve us during the journey, though these attentions were in no way connected with his duty. The generosity and nobility of his conduct moved us to tears.
>
> (Golownin, 1824b, p. 61)

Captain Golownin's witness of captivity conditions and practices in Ezo is very interesting. It stands in stark contrast to the views of American and British observers in a later period. For them the Japanese penal system was "barbarous" and an important reason to impose on the Japanese unequal treaties and related attempts to "rationalize" the penal system. It is to these developments that the next chapter turns.

Notes

1 Golownin writes "*ro*" but likely means the Japanese word "*rō*".
2 Golownin writes "*sagi*" but likely means the Japanese word "sake".

Bibliography

Botsman, D.V. 1992, Punishment and Power in the Tokugawa Period. *East Asian History*, 3, pp. 1–32.

Botsman, D.V. 1999, *Crime, Punishment and the Making of Modern Japan, 1790–1895*. Phil. Diss., Princeton University Press.

Botsman, D.V. 2014, Of Pity and Poison: Imprisoning Women in Modern Japan. In Burns, S.L. and Brooks, B.J. eds. *Gender and Law in the Japanese Imperium*. Honolulu: University of Hawaii Press, pp. 136–158.

Boxer, C.R. 1993, *The Christian Century in Japan 1549–1650*. Manchester: Carcanet Press.

Cieslik, G. 1941, Review: Ezo Kirishitan-shi (Geschichte des Christentums in Ezo). by Gerhard, Huber. *Monumenta Nipponica*, 4/1, pp. 320–321.

Enomoto, M. 1999, *Hokkaido no rekishi*. Sapporo: Hokkaido shinbunsha.

Golownin, V.M. 1824a, *Memoirs of a Captivity in Japan, During the Years 1811, 1812, and 1813: With Observations on the Country and People. Vol. 1*. London: Henry Colburn & Co.

Golownin, V.M. 1824b, *Memoirs of a Captivity in Japan, During the Years 1811, 1812, and 1813: With Observations on the Country and People. Vol. 2*. London: Henry Colburn & Co.

Hall, J.W. 1955, *Tanuma Okitsugu, 1719–1788: Forerunner of Modern Japan*. Cambridge: Harvard University Press.

Hall, J.W. 2008, Introduction. In Hall, J.W. ed. *The Cambridge History of Japan. Vol. 4: Early Modern Japan*. Cambridge: Cambridge University Press, pp. 1–39.

Hiramatsu, Y. 1994, *Edo no tsumi to batsu*. Tokyo: Heibonsha.

Huber, G. 1973 [¹1939], *Ezo Kirishitanshi*. Sapporo: Hokkaido henshu senta.

Martinez, D. 1756, *Compendio Histórico de la Apostolica Provincia de San Gregorio de Philipinas, de Religiosos descalzos de N.P. San Francisco*. Madrid: En la Imprenta de la Viuda de Manuel Fernandez y del Supremo Consejo de la Inquisicion.

Nakagawara, T. 1988, *Kinsei Hokkaido gyō keishi*. Tokyo: Dōsei.

Oguma, E. 2017, *The Boundaries of 'the Japanese': Vol. 2. Korea, Taiwan and the Ainu 1868–1945*. Melbourne: Trans Pacific Press.

Shigematsu, K. 2005, *Nihon gokuseishi no kenkyū*. Tokyo: Yoshikawa Kōbunkan.

Shigematsu, K. 2011, *Nihon runintōshi: Sono tayōsei to keibatsu no jidaiteki tokusei*. Tokyo: Fuji shuppan.

Tsukada, T. 1995, Kinsei no mushuku to ninsoku yoseba. In Yasumaru, Y. ed. *Kangoku no tanjō*. Tokyo and Osaka: Asahi shinbunsha.

2 Hokkaido prison island

In the wake of the Meiji Restoration and the imposition of a series of unequal treaties by foreign Western countries on Japan, legal reform became a political priority for the new Meiji government. During this process, the northern-most island's significance as a place of political exile and banishment was reinforced through the establishment of three *shūjikan* (central prisons) on Hokkaido. Although initially conceptualized to address the rising numbers of political convicts, the *shūjikan* were also used for convicts whose sentence was for at least 12 years of imprisonment with forced labour.

"Civilizing" the penal system

Even before the "opening" up of Japan in 1854, there were several European reports of the cruel persecution of Christians from the 16th century onwards (e.g. Martinez, 1756; Rodrigues, 1630). The barbarity of *Japanese* punishments, however, only became common knowledge in Europe in the 19th century. By this time, public executions had been banned in Europe, and against the backdrop of the so-called "Unequal Treaties", the issue of reforming Japanese penal law became increasingly urgent because the Western powers regarded the legal system of a nation as an indication of its "level of civilization".

Statehood alone was insufficient for a nation to be recognized as a legal subject of international law, as jurist Lassa Oppenheim notes in his 1920 book, *International Law*. Admission into the "family of nations" could only be achieved when all "civilized" nations recognized the state in question. In addition to Western European states and Christian nations which had developed outside Europe, Oppenheim includes Japan and Turkey as the only non-European, non-Christian states in the "family of nations" list (Anaya, 1996, p. 21).

By this time, Japan had obviously succeeded in securing its place within the international community. The path leading to this recognition, however, was marked by a fundamental restructuring of Japanese society, politics, culture and economy, as well as its military interventions. Within this context, the reform of the penal system was a key challenge for the Meiji government. The problem was how to abolish the old, "barbaric" customs and replace them with "humane" criminal laws in line with Western standards. Many Western observers were horrified at Japanese punishments such as disembowelment. Additionally, Western perception of anti-foreign attitudes among the Japanese intensified Western nations' unease towards Japan. For example, the British diplomat Ernest Satow who spent two decades in Japan, from 1862 to 1882, noted in his recollections:

> Japan came to be known as a country where the foreigner carried his life in his hand. (. . .) Even in England before I left to take up my appointment, we felt that apart from the chances of climate, the risk of coming to an untimely end at the hands of an expert swordsman must be taken into account.
>
> (Satow, 1983, p. 47)

These circumstances also served as the background for the enforcement of the so-called "extraterritoriality clause" in the Kanagawa Treaty (1854). This special regulation imposed on Japan stipulated that in the case of a legal transgression, Western visitors were not answerable to a Japanese court but to a court comprising the foreign community in Japan (Botsman, 1999, p. 253). The abolishment of the unequal treaties was indeed one of the political priorities of the Meiji government and therefore it was eager to reform penal law.

Following the establishment of the new government in 1868, it immediately abolished all sentences of banishment, replacing them with imprisonment with forced labour. In that same year, all sentences of exile were limited to the island of Ezo, and the execution of the death penalty was subjected to sanction by the Office of Penal Law, which had been created for this very task (*keihō jimu sōtoku*; this became the Ministry of Justice, *gyōbusho*, in 1869), and two of the most spectacular death penalties were abolished (death at the stake and crucifixion) or at least restricted to regicide and patricide (Botsman, 1999, p. 263). These changes are significant insofar as they illustrate how the open display of executions was clearly constrained and imprisonment became more important as a sentence. Proclaiming Ezo to be the only place of exile is also significant, as the decision foreshadowed Hokkaido's leading role as a "prisoners' island" in the years to come.

In 1870 the new edition of penal law (*Shinritsu kōryō*) came into effect. For several reasons, however, it did not immediately lead to the extraterritoriality clause being abolished. The new penal law's wording was still similar to ancient Chinese legal texts, and punishments continued to be classified in the same five categories as had been used since antiquity: flogging, severe flogging, hard labour for one to three years, exile and death. In addition, the *Shinritsu kōryō* provided for class privilege to be upheld in penal law (Yasumaru, 1995, pp. 39–40).

The first Meiji official to conduct a thorough modernization of the Japanese penal system was Ohara Shigeya. Ohara was born in 1834 to a samurai family in Okayama domain. In his youth he had spent time in an arrest house for alleged involvement in acts of treason. However, after the Meiji Ishin, the new government appointed him as domain representative. He also became a judge in the Office of Criminal Law. Based on his own experiences, he submitted a critical appraisal of the national convict houses to the Ministry of Justice, in which he denounced the *rōnanushi* system and its unsanitary conditions and advocated for prison reform based on the Western model. In 1870, Ohara was sent on a study trip to the British colonies of Singapore and Hong Kong to obtain a first-hand impression of Western prison institutions. After returning to Japan in late 1871, Ohara worked on recording his observations and wrote his famous illustrated *Prison Regulations* (*Kangoku soku narabi ni zushiki*), which he submitted to the reformist Minister of the Interior, Etō Shinpei, as Japan's first modern prison regime in 1872. The prison regime's rules featured ideas similar to Jeremy Bentham's panopticon. However, Ohara also conceived of prison as a space of healing and included the planting of pharmaceutical plants such as hibiscus (Maeda, 2004, pp. 31–32). Although the prompt implementation of the draft failed – mainly for budgetary reasons – Ohara had succeeded in outlining the theoretical framework of modern prisons in Japan (Shigematsu, 1985, pp. 4–5).

In 1873, the state's efforts at reform were resumed in the form of a revision of penal law. The five traditional categories of punishment were abolished and replaced by imprisonment with hard labour and the death penalty. This key role of imprisonment not only meant a massive restriction and rationalization of the register of punishment, but it also brought an evermore pressing need for suitable penal institutions in order to enforce sentences (Yasumaru, 1995, p. 40).

In 1875, the French legal expert Gustave Emile Boissonade de Fontarabie vehemently advocated the abolition of torture. An adviser to the Meiji regime, he emphasized in his *Mémoire sur l'abolition de la torture* (Report on the Abolition of Torture) that lifting the "Unequal Treaties" was linked to renouncing the use of torture. However, it was not foreign pressure alone that contributed to the official abolition of torture in Japan. As it was not enforced until 1879, the more important reason behind this development seems to be the establishment of a functioning police apparatus and judiciary, which had already been completed at the time. Policies of deterrence could thus be replaced by those of social control.

Boissonade's activities, however, did not end with his commitment to ending torture. Under his direction, the first Japanese legal code following Western principles was finally drafted, closely modelled after its French counterpart, coming into effect in 1880. Punishment according to social status was now finally abolished, and the death sentence was restricted to death by hanging behind prison walls. All punishments – apart from fines – now also contained some form of detention: forced labour, banishment, detention in combination with hard labour, and normal detention, with forced labour and banishment only permissible on islands (Botsman, 1999, pp. 309–310). Banishment, in particular, was used for the rising numbers of political convicts.

Political uprisings and the *shūjikan* system

The first years of the Meiji period were marked by widespread social unrest and political uprisings. The protagonists of these various movements were mainly peasants, former samurai (*shizoku*), and members of the Movement for Freedom and Peoples's Rights (*Jiyū minken undō*).

During the early Meiji period, peasant uprisings reached their peak in 1869 with 110 uprisings. Half of these movements were in response to village headmen who committed wrongdoings and complications in landlord-tenant relations. The other half were mostly caused by the imposition of land tax. However, the Meiji government did not react to these movements by detaining participants (Vlastos, 2008, p. 368). In contrast to these rural movements, the *shizuko* revolts by former samurai were armed uprisings that threatened to overthrow the Meiji government. The main reason for this unrest was the deteriorating living conditions of the samurai. The leaders of the *shizuko* movements were all young samurai from southwestern Japan. Eto Shinpei, Maebara Issei and Saigō Takamori were leaders of the largest revolts. They had all served the Meiji government in the Council of State (Dajokan) and identified a great deal with the imperial cause. Starting with the Saga Rebellion of 1874, this armed opposition against the Meiji government grew and culminated in the Satsuma Rebellion (*Seinan Sensō*) of 1877 (Vlastos, 2008, pp. 382–385). Indeed, the Satsuma Rebellion (*Seinan Sensō*) under the leadership of Saigō Takamori was the largest samurai uprising. As a consequence, 43,000 individuals were arrested, with 2,764 being executed and 27,000 sentenced to detention and forced labour (Mitchell, 1992, pp. 15–17). Thus, from the 1877 Satsuma Rebellion onwards, the number of political convicts rose steadily. The existing prison system was not equipped for rising numbers of political offenders. As a result, the Ministry of the Interior drafted a plan to build a large, new type of prison – a *shūjikan* (gather-and-control prison) – in the northern prefecture of Miyagi. This location recommended itself by its great distance from the centre of unrest in Kyūshū and by the possibility it presented for putting a large number of people to work at tasks like cutting slate. For the prison construction, 301 officers of Saigō's army were dispensed to Sendai in 1877, where they worked for two years on finishing the building while being housed in former convict houses. The architecture of the Miyagi prison resembled the penitentiary in Leuven, Belgium, the only difference being that it was made from wood, not stone (Shigematsu, 1985, p. 93). In 1878 another *shūjikan* was built in the Tokyo district of Kosuge. Its location was strategically chosen to be directly adjacent to the Tokyo brickworks. When the private entrepreneur of these works encountered financial difficulties, the Ministry of the Interior decided to include the factory as part of the prison. The result was Japan's first "prison factory". Although the Kosuge prison was only completely finished in 1888, it was presented abroad from 1879 as the first large-scale Japanese national convict house, together with Miyagi Prison (Shigematsu, 1985, pp. 68–71).

The decision to build large-scale prisons on Hokkaido was directly related to all these wider political uprisings and movements. In 1878, the Japanese Senate discussed how to deal with political convicts, with an agreement reached to send them to be incarcerated on islands. This provision goes back to Japan's long tradition of sending political exiles to live on islands (Shigematsu, 2011). There were also similar rules in the French Code Pénal (1810) according to which the banishment to another country (outside the French Empire) was reserved for political criminals (O'Brian, 1982, p. 26).

However, Interior Minister Itō Hirobumi had considerable concerns about this proposal as the available island locations were generally small areas with few work opportunities. In a letter dated 17 September 1879, he turned to Sanjō Sanetomi, Director of the Council of State (Dajōkan), alerting him to the content of the new criminal code that was to come into effect a year later. Some 2,000 individuals were already marked for a 12-year island banishment with forced labour sentence. Apparently projecting that this number would remain stable over the following years, Itō argued that a future scenario of 24,000 prisoners with sentences of 12–15 years would create a mass of people who could not possibly be accommodated or employed on the usual islands of banishment (Itō, as cited in Shigematsu, 1970, p. 121). Itō's letter ends with the proposed solution of establishing Hokkaido as a prison island:

> Therefore, I think that the prisoners should be transported to Hokkaido. The climate and soil of Hokkaido are different from other regions, but there are hundreds of *ri* [1 ri = 3.9 km; P.J.] of fertile land that the prisoners could reclaim, or they could work in mining. On days when it is extremely cold and [the earth; P.J.] hard, they can be tasked with

suitable activities. When the deportees, or those sentenced to forced labour, are discharged, they will be made to work in agriculture, or to work in a craft, and their numbers will slowly increase over the years.

(Itō, cited in Shigematsu, 1970, p. 122)

It appears Itō successfully won over Sanjō to this idea. On 1 February 1880, Sanjō decided to establish prisons on Hokkaido (HKK, 1989, p. 33). Subsequently, on 26 February 1880, Itō asked Kuroda Kiyotaki at the Kaitaku-shi for his cooperation:

> Our aim is to send prisoners to Hokkaido. By having prisoners do work that serves the noble cause of development, they will acquire the ability to better themselves. In the future, they will contribute to the public welfare and rehabilitated prisoners will be brought to develop a region based on an independent economy.
>
> (Itō, as cited in Shigematsu, 1970, p. 122)

The decision to use Hokkaido enabled the Interior Minister to "kill three birds with one stone" (*isseki sanchō*). Firstly, it afforded an opportunity for the government to send all political convicts to the outermost periphery. There, these prisoners would earn their living by subsistence farming, at little cost to the government. Secondly, land development on the island, which had been sluggish anyway, could be stimulated with a mass of cheap labour. And thirdly, there was hope that discharged and reformed prisoners would settle on Hokkaido and contribute to the population growth of this sparsely populated area by working and starting families there (Iida, 1997, p. 18; Shigematsu, 1970, p. 122).

The *Kaitaku-shi* was charged with proposing suitable locations for the first prison building and the initial sum of 100,000 yen was put aside for its establishment. Three prospective building sites were identified: the first was Shibetsuputo in the Kabato-*gun* (Ishikari-*kuni*) to the north of Ishikari River, the second in the region at the foot of Mount Shiribeshi (today: Yōteizan) on the border between Shiribeshi and Iburi, and the third at the coast near the mouth of Tokachi River. In April 1880, Tsukigata Kiyoshi, an official of the Ministry of the Interior, was commissioned with the final decision and sent on an expedition to Hokkaido. In his report *Hokkai kaiyū ki* (Notes of a Tour of the Northern Sea), Tsukigata argued against the regions of Shiribeshi and Tokachi, as these locations were less conveniently situated for transport and because people had already settled in the immediate vicinity. Arguments in favour of Shibetsuputo were its strategic proximity to cities like Sapporo and Tōbetsu, as well as the existence of a waterway for transport (Shigematsu, 1970, pp. 126–127). By August the following year, the prison building was already finished and officially opened on 3 September 1881 (Shigematsu, 1970, p. 130).

In the meantime, Matsukata Masayoshi (Minister of Finance from November 1881) had started to bring his influence to bear on the government's prison construction plans. In a letter to Sanjō in November 1880, before the prison on Hokkaido had even been built, he proposed reducing the number of buildings planned for the first Hokkaido prison, and cutting the funds by half. Three months later, this proposal was accepted (Hosokawa, 1997, pp. 60–61). On 7 April 1881, Matsukata again applied to the Dajōkan Council, proposing to use the budget allocated to the prison buildings in Kyūshū and Chūgoku for the further construction of central prisons on Hokkaido. The idea was that, given the increasing numbers of political prisoners to 4,000, it was advisable to invest more money in the construction of prisons on the island of Hokkaido instead. Matsukata argued that the benefits of future employment of prisoners would include a quick colonization of Hokkaido (Matsukata, as cited in Hosokawa, 1997, p. 61). This proposal, too, was accepted in June that same year (Hosokawa, 1997, p. 62).

Political prisoners

Who were these political convicts who were sent to prisons in Hokkaido? Many of them were members of the Freedom and People's Rights Movement. The movement promoted liberty, equality and the right to an elected government, and members included intellectuals and former leaders of the Meiji Restoration from both urban and rural areas. They comprised people of different social status such as *shizuko*, poor farmers and wealthy commoners (Vlastos, 2008, p. 402). As the Freedom and People's Rights Movement gained in membership, the Meiji government began to restrict citizens' rights to freedom of expression. The movement opposed the government in a number of violent uprisings, and consequently increasing numbers of supporters were arrested and sent to Hokkaido's Kabato, Sorachi and Kushiro Prisons.

It is estimated that in 1875, 60 members were arrested compared to more than 300 in 1880. In 1881 the movement officially became the Liberal Party (Jiyūtō). The Fukushima incident of 1882 marked the radicalization of the democratic movement as supporters protested against the repressive policies of Governor Mishima Michitsune. During the crackdown of the uprising, 1,000 members and sympathizers of the Liberal Party were arrested and tortured. Fifty-seven party members were charged with treason, and Kōno Hiromi was charged with conspiracy to overthrow the government and sentenced to 7 years in Sorachi Prison.

The Kabasan incident (September 1884) was an attempt by 16 people to assassinate Michishima Michitsune as revenge for the brutal crackdown of the 1882 Fukushima incident. It was the first time during the Meiji period that bombs were used for revolutionary purposes (Bowen, 1976, p. 46).

Koinuma Kuhachirō, the 34-year-old leader of the Kabasan incident, was sent to Sorachi Prison, while Kusano Sakuma and Isogawa Motokichi, both 19 years old, were sent to Kabato Prison.

The Chichibu incident (November 1884) was a large-scale violent reaction against economic distress. It was the largest incident of the Jiyūtō and involved 5,000–10,000 people (depending on different estimates), of whom 4,000 were found guilty. Three hundred were declared felons and seven leaders were sentenced to death (Irokawa, 1985, p. 154; Oda, 2016, p. 130, Vlastos, 2008, pp. 416–418). Several protagonists of the Chichibu incident were sent to prisons in Hokkaido. Kakizaki Yoshifuji and Ōno Chōshirō, for instance, were sent to Kabato Prison. Kakizaki was working for the Konmintō (Poor People's Party) collecting weapons and financial resources. He was arrested and sentenced to lifelong imprisonment because he burned a house belonging to a moneylender. In 1886, he died of cardiac arrest in Kabato Prison and was buried in its grounds. Ōno was also a member of the Poor People's Party and worked for Kikuchi Kampei, one of the leaders of the Chichibu incident (Koike, 1981, pp. 22–23; Wakabayashi, 2012, pp. 118–119). Kikuchi himself escaped to Nagano where he was arrested 2 years later and sent to Kabato. However, in 1889 he was given amnesty and released. Eventually he was sent to Abashiri Prison for another reason in 1905 where he spent 20 years of his life (Irokawa, 1985, p. 157; Koike, 1981, pp. 12–13; Kumagai, 1992, pp. 51–52). Inoue Denzō, one of the leaders of the Chichibu incident who was sentenced to death, fled alone in 1887 to Hokkaido. There, he adopted a new name and identity and worked at various places such as Ishikari and Sapporo before he eventually settled in Kitami. He kept his involvement in the Chichibu incident a secret even from his family, only revealing his past to them shortly before his death in 1918 (Oda, 2016, p. 130).

In Hokkaido, political prisoners were treated with respect. For example, after his involvement in the Shizuoka Incident (1886), Nakano Jirosaburō was arrested and sentenced to 14 years' imprisonment and penal servitude. When he was sent to Sorachi Prison, his wife Ito decided to join him in Hokkaido, entrusting their children to her ageing mother. She moved to Sapporo where she opened a hairdressing business and was able to visit her husband regularly at Sorachi Prison. Prison Director Watanabe Koreaki knew of these visits and even supported Nakano's wife with gifts of cash and other goods (Wakabayashi, 2012, p. 120).

However, the gradual radicalization of the Freedom and People's Rights Movement changed the practice of sending mostly political convicts to Hokkaido. From 1881 onwards, the Meiji government ceased to distinguish political from non-political convicts and so sent increasing numbers of serious criminal offenders to Hokkaido (Anderson *et al.*, 2015, p. 153). And so it was that both political and non-political convicts were forced to work in the colonization of Hokkaido.

Bibliography

Anaya, S.J. 1996, *Indigenous People in International Law*. New York and Oxford: Oxford University Press.
Anderson, C. et al. 2015, Locating Penal Transportation: Punishment, Space, and Place c. 1750 to 1900. In Morin, K.M. and Moran, D. eds. *Historical Geographies of Prisons. Unlocking the Usable Carceral Past*. Abingdon and New York: Routledge, pp. 147–167.
Botsman, D.V. 1999, *Crime, Punishment and the Making of Modern Japan, 1790–1895*. Phil. Diss., Princeton University Press.
Bowen, R.W. 1976, *Rebellion and Democracy: A Study of Commoners in the Popular Rights Movement of the Early Meiji Period*. Phil. Diss., University of British Columbia.
HKK = Hokkaido kaitaku kinenkan, ed. 1989, *Shūjikan. Kaitaku to shūjinrō dō*. Sapporo: Hokkaido kaitaku kinenkan.
Hosokawa, K. 1997, Meiji zenki no Hokkaido shūjikan. In Takashio, H. and Nakayama, K. eds. *Hokkaido shūjikan ronkō*. Tokyo: Kōbundō, pp. 59–74.
Iida, M. 1997, Hokkaidō no ayumi to shūjikan. In Takashio H. and Nakayam K. eds. *Hokkaidō shūjikan ronkō*. Tokyo: Kōbundō.
Irokawa, D. 1985, *The Culture of the Meiji Period*. Princeton: Princeton University Press.
Koike, Y. 1981 [¹1973], *Kusaritsuka. Jiyūminken to shūjin rōdō no kiroku*. Tokyo: Gendaishi shuppankai.
Kumagai, S. 1992, *Kabato kangoku*. Sapporo: Hokkaido Shinbunsha.
Maeda, A. 2004, Utopia of the Prisonhouse: A Reading of *In Darkest Tokyo*. In Fuji, J.A. ed. *Text and the City: Essays on Japanese Modernity*. Durham and London: Duke University Press, pp. 21–64.
Martinez, D. 1756, *Compendio Histórico de la Apostolica Provincia de San Gregorio de Philipinas, de Religiosos descalzos de N.P. San Francisco*. Madrid: En la Imprenta de la Viuda de Manuel Fernandez y del Supremo Consejo de la Inquisicion.
Mitchell, R.H. 1992, *Janus-Faced Justice: Political Crimes in Imperial Japan*. Honolulu: University of Hawaii Press.
O'Brian, P. 1982, *The Promise of Punishment: Prisons in Nineteenth-Century France*. Princeton: Princeton University Press.
Oda, H. 2016, Unearthing the History of *minshū* in Hokkaido: The Case Study of the Okhotsk People's History Workshop. In Seaton, P. ed. *Local History and War Memories in Hokkaido*. London: Routledge, pp. 129–158.
Rodrigues, J. 1630, *The Palme of Christian Fortitude: Or the Glorious Combats of Christians in Iaponia: Taken Out of Letters of the Society of Iesus from*

Thence Anno 1624. [electronic resource]. [Saint-Omer: Printed by the widow of C. Boscard] With permission of superiours.

Satow, E.M. 1983, *A Diplomat in Japan: An Inner History of the Japanese Reformation*. Tokyo: Tuttle.

Shigematsu, K. 1970, *Hokkaido gyō keishi*. Tokyo: Zufu shuppan.

Shigematsu, K. 1985, *Zukan Nihon no kangokushi*. Tokyo: Yūzankaku shuppan.

Shigematsu, K. 2011, *Nihon runintōshi: Sono tayōsei to keibatsu no jidaiteki tokusei*. Tokyo: Fuji shuppan.

Vlastos, S. 2008, Opposition Movements in Early Meiji, 1868–1885. In Jansen, M.B. ed. *The Cambridge History of Japan. Vol. 5*. Cambridge: Cambridge University Press, pp. 367–431.

Wakabayashi, S. 2012, *Rukei chi naku*. Sapporo: Nakanishi Shuppan.

Yasumaru, Y. 1995, *Kangoku no tanjō*. Tokyo and Osaka: Asahi shinbunsha.

3 Prisons and rural development, 1881–1886

This chapter addresses the events surrounding the establishment of the three large central prisons of Hokkaido: Kabato, Sorachi and Kushiro. We explain the role these prisons played among the surrounding settler communities and examines the characteristics of convict labour during the period from 1881 to 1886. Findings suggest that during this period prisoners were mostly engaged in rural development.

Kabato Prison

After Shibetsuputo was selected as the location of Hokkaido's first central penitentiary and its construction work finished in record time, Kabato Prison was opened on 2 September 1881. During the festivities, the place name was changed, in honour of its "founder" Tsukigata Kyoshi, from Shibetsuputo in the Ainu language to Tsukigata, a name it still bears today. Tsukigata had served with government forces during the *Seinan Sensō* (Satsuma Rebellion), and was now appointed the first warden of Kabato Prison to administer a penal institution built for political prisoners (Botsman, 2005, p. 167; Shigematsu, 1970, p. 130).

For financial reasons, the initial plans to allow 11,000 *tsubo* (approx. 36,410 sq. m) for the living quarters of the 3,000 inmates were not realized (Nagai and Ōba, 1999, p. 93). Instead, the entire prison covered a total area of 7,386 *tsubo* (approx. 24,448 sq. m). This extensive complex contained detention rooms as well as an additional 94 administrative buildings. In general, the prisoners were quartered in wooden barracks with no natural light. Confinement in one of the nine solitary barracks was regarded as additional punishment. The quarters for the religious prison ministers were situated between the group barracks and the solitary sheds. In addition to these units, there was also a factory block and an administrative area, with the entire facility surrounded by a 15-centimetre thick and 5.5-metre high black fence (Shigematsu, 1970, p. 130).

During its initial years, Kabato Prison had a lot of contact with the surrounding communities. Tsukigata Kiyoshi's function was not restricted to managing Kabato Prison. He was also the highest administrative official of the three *gun*, Kabato, Uryū and Kamigawa. From 1882 onwards he was also the head of the mail service and local police force. Forms of address like "*tengoku-sama*" (Mr Prison Warden) or "*tengoku kakka*" (his Excellency, the prison warden) used for Tsukigata during his public appearances testify to the prison warden's important role in the region at this time (Shigematsu, 1970, p. 227).

Because of the various additional offices of its warden, the Kabato facility was initially also regarded as an important communication hub between Hokkaido and Tokyo. For example, orders from the Ministry of the Interior were communicated via the prison to the surrounding communities. In addition, settlers in the area used the prison's medical facilities. Although this phenomenon of settlers using the prison's clinic only lasted until the establishment of the Hokkaido-chō in 1886, the prison's socio-political role was significant enough for Shigematsu to call it a "period of prison rule" (*kangoku chisei*) over the area (Shigematsu, 1970, pp. 171–172).

The ratio of staff to inmates had been determined by the Ministry of the Interior before the facility had opened. There was to be five lower officials for an inmate population of fewer than 200, with one further official per 150 additional inmates. There was also one guard per 50 inmates. The only provision for the prison priest, medical doctor and teacher was that their wages were to be in line with that of the other staff. Finally, one assistant guard was to be hired for every 10 inmates. The assistant guards received a salary of less than 8 yen each, to be paid out on either a daily or monthly basis (Fujii, 1997, p. 100).

The recruitment of prison personnel was an important matter. In a letter to Sanjō dated 5 October 1881, Matsukata wrote:

> For the time being, we have mustered a hundred reserve guards and added seven head guards, and they are made to keep a very strict watch. At the same time, these fellows have been told to apply themselves to rural development. After all, if we promote the plan that they should, in the long run, settle here and provide for themselves, we will also meet the goals of the national economy, and can kill two birds with one. I will send a cost estimate in a separate letter.
>
> (Matsukata, as cited in Fujii, 1997, p. 103)

This letter clearly demonstrates that the authorities had potential colonizers in mind when recruiting prison guards. The presence of prisoners and prison staff on Hokkaido was therefore closely connected to the rural development of Hokkaido.

In December 1881, Kabato Prison finally obtained permission from the Ministry of the Interior to recruit three additional head guards and 50 regular guards (Fujii, 1997, p. 104). Interestingly, most of the guards employed at Kabato, like the majority of other immigrants to Hokkaido, originally came from the prefectures of Sendai and Akita (Shigematsu, 1970, p. 148), regions traditionally faithful to the *bakufu* who had been on the losing side of the Boshin War (1868–1869).

The increase in recruitment during Kabato Prison's first months must also be understood in relation to inmate numbers, which were considerably higher than originally expected. Even before the facility was officially opened, 39 prisoners had arrived, followed by another 300 two weeks later in mid-September. These groups of convicts had been gathered by the police headquartered in Osaka and two other prefectures and were shipped to Otaru guarded by three or four prison officials. After a night spent in Otaru, they were transported to Kabato the following day. In November that same year, another 160 people were sent to Kabato, resulting in the number of inmates reaching a total of nearly 500 only two months after the prison was opened. As this was 100 more convicts than projected for the initial phase, it was necessary for the government to respond quickly with special measures and personnel recruitment, as well as with additional funding (Yamada, 1997, pp. 176–177). A year later, the number of inmates again increased by another 500 (KSER, 1993 [1887], p. 509) and steadily rose over the following years due to the growing arrests of political activists. The inmates were mostly put to work in agricultural and industrial activities.

Agricultural activities

Although the other two central prisons, Sorachi and Kushiro, were also active in agriculture, it was mainly the inmates of the Kabato facility who were ordered to do agricultural work. In particular, during the initial phase of the prison, clearing land and cultivating the soil constituted the main share of convict labour work (SECH, 1993 [1891], p. 374).

The land belonging to the Kabato Prison was divided into two agricultural areas which were first cleared by the inmates and then cultivated. One area, Shibetsu estate, was located in the immediate vicinity of the prison in Tōmanai (Tōsunai)[1] along the Ishikari River and worked on by around 200 convicts per day. The second area, Chiraiotsu estate, lay about 4 kilometres to the southwest of the prison. Unlike Shibetsu, two overnight camps for prisoners were built in Chiraiotsu. Each day, around 400 prisoners were forced to clear the forest and develop and cultivate the cleared land (Higashi, 1997, p. 310). Working conditions were poor. The prisoners had to clear high bamboo thickets that were difficult to cut down and allowed hardly any light through. In addition, the forced labourers encountered wild animals like brown bears and adders, and it was common for them to be attacked and bitten by swarms of gadflies (Shigematsu, 1970, p. 133). To make matters worse, the weather was extremely cold and dark:

> The sky is always cloudy, there is a perpetual low-lying mist. It is not uncommon to not see a single ray of sun for ten days at a time. In October, frost comes early and is severe, the trees die, and a biting wind rises. In late October or early November, it starts to snow, the water freezes, the mountain streams become white all at once, and a silvery world is revealed. From then on, the snowfall never stops for nearly half a year. Travel across land or water is affected by the cold, and the thermometer drops to temperatures below zero degrees.
>
> (KSER, 1993 [1887], p. 508)

This description of the climatic conditions in the Ishikari region was also included in official reports to the Imperial Parliament. During the long winter period, the convicts mainly cut trees or were occupied with work behind the prison walls. During the summer months, it was possible to cultivate the developed land (Shigematsu, 1970, p. 132). The goal of all this work was to allow the government to sell the land to settlers after the convicts had finished the most difficult tasks, such as felling the trees and extracting deep roots (Koike, 1981, pp. 98–99).

The Chiraiotsu estate was declared a settlement area in April 1887, and a total of 232.4 ha of developed land and non-colonized regions were given to the Hokkaido-chō, which then sold the land to the Hokuetsu Shokuminsha settlers' organization.[2] Two years later, the Hokkaido-chō took over 73 ha of the Shibetsu estate and sold the property to the entrepreneur Tsuchida Masajirō (Higashi, 1997, p. 310). This means that Kabato Prison had, at this point, only 44.9 ha of land left. However, in the following two years, 1890–1891, convict land development was again initiated and, in 1892, the prison was able to report a total property of 105.9 ha land to the Imperial Parliament (SECH, 1993 [1891], p. 375).

Agricultural production by the Kabato facility increased alongside the progress of land development. Production started in 1884, with hemp being produced for fishing nets and different types of rope for use in the prison. From 1885 onwards, potatoes, horseradish, millet and barley were cultivated to feed the prisoners, as well as soybeans and wheat for the production of miso and soy sauce. In addition, oats were planted to feed horses and cattle. This relatively modest range was expanded the following year with rye, beets and cabbage for the prison's subsistence. There was also an attempt to cultivate indigo plants. In 1886, the cultivation of carrots, squash, black salsify and leeks likely brought some variety to the prisoners' diet. The following year, cultivation of rapeseed was started for the production of oil for the implements used in the facility. In 1890, buckwheat for farm horses and a new summer beet for the prisoners' subsistence were also planted (SECH, 1993 [1891], pp. 377–386).

From the annotations on contemporary statistics, it is clear that the Kabato Prison was trying to achieve subsistence farming. Its success over the years was doubtful: harvests were often affected by crop failure due to unfavourable weather conditions, plagues of insects or the unavailability of fertilizers. So, the prison repeatedly depended on food imports (mostly rice) from Honshū (Nasu, 1987, p. 44).

In spite of these rather unfortunate results in subsistence farming, by clearing large areas of land the convicts of Kabato Prison nevertheless carried out essential groundwork for subsequent settlers. The other prisons also contributed to land clearance on Hokkaido, if to a lesser extent, and estimates are that by 1898, a total land surface of 1,746,356 ha had been reclaimed by prisoners, most of which was passed on to immigrants (Higashi, 1997, p. 309).

Industrial activities

Primary sources enumerate a total of 18 different fields of industry at the Kabato facility (SECH, 1993 [1891], p. 388). Of these, the most important were wood processing, ironworks, joinery, charcoal burning and the production of miso and soy sauce (KSER, 1993 [1887], pp. 512–513).

As prison labour was mostly used in agriculture during the early years of the Kabato facility, industrial activities were initially developed according to agricultural production needs, for instance by producing implements and processing produce. Also, it is important to note that the majority of convicts did not have the necessary experience and skills to carry out industrial activities (Hosokawa, 1997b, p. 78). They needed training in these technical skills (KSER, 1993 [1887], p. 512): the ideal prisoner was to have skills that allowed management to use him like a skilled labourer, or rather, it was expected that his performance equalled that of a "free" labourer.

From 1881, around 20 inmates per day were put to work manufacturing everyday wooden objects for the prison such as braziers, doors, windows, barrels and boxes. In the following years, this workshop mainly produced basic commodities for the prison. At the same time, the number of external customers rose steadily. In spite of the demand for such wood products, the workshop lacked the financial means to procure raw material. Soit was privatized in 1884, although in 1886 it was again re-sold to the state. This change of ownership, however, did not entail any change in the nature of the work. Even after the business was privatized, it continued to use forced labour (SECH, 1993 [1891], p. 390).

The ironworks, too, were initially limited to the production of basic commodities, as establishing the industry involved high financial costs. When the procurement of raw material became easier, the focus of prisoners' activities shifted to the production of mainly agricultural implements (although the workshops also accepted commissions from outside the prison). Production in the prison-owned workshop enabled the facility to save a large sum of money which would otherwise have been needed to purchase finished implements imported from other regions (Hosokawa, 1997b, p. 79).

The production of wooden boards was another important industrial activity. In this area, in particular, the convict labourers needed special training and skill:

> As the training of the workers was not yet satisfactory, and there were no trainers either, it was not possible to produce good articles. But by mutually encouraging each other and recently also by exercising their duties without laziness, the prison labourers have succeeded in producing articles that are not inferior to those offered on the market in the city.
>
> (KSER, 1993 [1887], p. 514)

This quotation demonstrates the problem mentioned earlier: the insufficient training of the convict labourers and the effect this had on the products they could make. As it is likely that only very few inmates had been apprenticed in carpentry before being interred, the prison management had to train its producers itself. In the case of this form of work, the training of prisoners appeared to have paid off for the facility. The influx of new prison staff and especially of settlers required the construction of new houses, and thus increased demand for cheap carpentry work which the trained prisoners could provide. The prisoners who worked in this field were also indispensable for making all the repairs to the prison buildings themselves (KSER, 1993 [1887], p. 514).

The charcoal burning industry was likewise established with difficulty and great initial trouble. An additional factor was the unfavourable soil conditions, which resulted in the failure of all initial efforts and led to concerns about the insecure heating situation. In the first winter after the Kabato facility was built, prisoners collected firewood in heavy snowfall and on frozen earth. They also attempted – unsuccessfully – to burn coal. Faced with this predicament, the prison management decided to construct a new furnace, which delivered better results. In 1882, the management recruited skilled charcoal burners, who trained the prisoners to work with the new furnace. Charcoal burning finally proceeded smoothly, and for two years enough coal was produced for the prison's use (KSER, 1993 [1887], pp. 514–515). However, due to the shortage of raw materials in 1884, coal production was moved to a specially built workshop in the village of Osokinai to the northeast of Tsukigata. This location had the disadvantage of having a long transport route between the prison and the production site, so the workshop was moved for a second time in 1888, to Horobinai, where an average of 40 prisoners worked on 15 coal burners over the following years (SECH, 1993 [1891], p. 388).

Finally, the prison also owned a miso and soy sauce brewery, the fifth area of activity dating from the initial prison operation phase. In contrast to the other four industries, the brewery was only taken on as a trial, in June 1882. The prison management bought a brewery that had been built and equipped with the necessary implements by the former Kaitaku-shi in the village of Shinoro, located about 66 kilometres (17 *ri*) from the prison. After necessary renovations to the site, provisional prisoners' barracks were built. These housings helped to ensure the efficient employment of the prison labour by avoiding unnecessary transportation to and from the work site. The amount of miso and soy sauce produced from the prison-owned agricultural estates' harvests was enough to supply the prison's needs. In some years, it was even possible to sell surplus product to merchants in Sapporo, Otaru and the Ishikari region. The brewery did not encounter any serious problems until the aforementioned sale of the Chiraiotsu estate in 1887 led to a significant decline in prison-owned agricultural production. With the estate's sale, it would have become necessary to import the required ingredients for miso and soy production at a high cost from other villages. As a consequence, the brewery was shut down in November 1887 and taken over by the Hokkaido-chō. However, the prison management was unwilling to do without the cost-saving products from in-house production and so built a manufacturing site on prison premises the next year, where prisoners continued to produce miso and soy sauce (SECH, 1993 [1891], p. 391).

In addition to the industrial activities described earlier, a number of other "light labour" (*keieki*) activities were added over the years (KSER, 1993 [1887], p. 515). For example, in October 1881, only a month after Kabato Prison opened, 25 prisoners were occupied daily with sewing work. They mainly produced uniforms for the guards and convicts, but external commissions were also accepted. Staff were dressed in the Western style, while the inmates were fitted with traditional Japanese convict uniforms (SECH, 1993 [1891], p. 387).

In that same month, a straw-weaving workshop was also established for the production of hiking sandals. As the raw material was imported from northern Niigata at relatively high cost, and the revenues hardly covered the cost of production, this activity was not a particularly profitable one (SECH, 1993 [1891], p. 393).

From November 1881, inmates also started producing the covering of sliding doors, for the prison as well as for private residences. However, this workshop was also privatized, together with the aforementioned carpentry workshop, in 1884, and transferred back to the state in 1886 (SECH, 1993 [1891], p. 391).

In addition, a barrel workshop, a shoe manufacture, a basketry and rope production as well as a dye works were established. Prisoners occupied in all of these industries mainly produced items for use by the facility (SECH, 1993 [1891], pp. 388; 392–393). There was also a short-lived attempt to put the prisoners to work in brickmaking. However, the project was quickly dropped due to technical deficiencies and a lack of prisoner training (SECH, 1993 [1891], p. 388). From 1885, the prisoners also contributed to internal clothing production by pulling cotton, and as of 1888, prison labour added to the paper stocks of the Kabato facility through paper production (SECH, 1993 [1891], pp. 392–393).

Except during the short-term privatization of the carpentry, tailoring and barrel-making workshops, and the shoe manufacture from 1884 to 1886, all these operations were managed by the prison authorities. In December 1889, entrepreneur Tsuchida Masajirō took over the four manufactures just mentioned, while submitting to the government a request to employ more prisoners (SECH, 1993 [1891], p. 389).

This outline of the industrial activities performed by the Kabato Prison inmates provides insight into the numerous activities of the prison workshops. It allows us to illustrate two aspects addressed in the theory section of this study with concrete examples. The notes on the tailor's workshop in contemporary sources provide information on the difference in dress between staff and prisoners. While the prison staff were dressed in the Western style, the prisoners were still clothed in the traditional Japanese manner. This policy fits in with the characteristics of total institutions, which draw clear lines of demarcation between the world of the staff and the world of the inmates, in order to reify the difference in authority: "In total institutions, there is a basic split between a large, managed group, conveniently called 'inmates', and a small supervisory staff" (Goffman, 1991, p. 18). To some extent, the guards serve as a daily reminder of the personified institution. In this way two different social and cultural worlds develop, "jogging alongside each other with points of official contact but little mutual penetration" (Goffman, 1991, p. 20) and "the institutional plant and name come to be identified by both staff and inmates as somehow belonging to staff" (Goffman, 1991, p. 20). In our case, the guards in Western uniform symbolize the principle of the modern penal institution, and in their appearance clearly demarcate themselves from the prisoners in Japanese dress.

The examination of the sources shows another essential characteristic of modern prisons: the twin functions of the penal institution to have, on the one hand, products made by the hands of prisoners and, on the other, to produce working prisoners (Foucault, 1991, p. 242). The inmates of the Kabato facility not only produced a wide range of agricultural implements and everyday commodities but, when necessary, they were also trained as skilled workers. When the performance of the forced labourers was equal to those of "free" workers, they were also employed by private individuals and the goods they produced were sold. Finally, the example of the entrepreneur Tsuchida demonstrates how the output of forced labourers was utilized by private businesses.

Sorachi Prison

Interior Minister Matsukata Masayoshi contemplated the plan to build further prisons on Hokkaido for the first time in 1881. He proposed this idea in a letter to the director of the Dajōkan, Sanjō Sanetomi, on 7 April 1881. The plan was approved in June that same year (Hosokawa, 1997a, pp. 61–62). As mentioned before, the essential idea was to halt the construction plans for two prisons in Kyūshū and Chūgoku and instead invest in prisons in peripheral Hokkaido, which seemed a particularly favourable space of exile for political prisoners.

The decision for the village of Ichikishiri (today, Mikasa) in Sorachi-*gun* as a location for the second central prison on Hokkaido was undoubtedly also linked to the coal deposits in nearby Horonai, and the possibilities for the intensive deployment of prisoners there. A year before the opening of Sorachi Prison, Yamanouchi Teiun, Director of the Office of Mining (*Baiden kaisai jimukyoku*), proposed to put prisoners to work at this coal mine (HKK, 1989, p. 16).

The Meiji government welcomed this idea. On 15 June 1882, Watanabe Koreaki, Secretary of the Interior Ministry, was already appointed prison warden. On 5 July 1882, the facility was opened and 70 convicts were received. They were immediately deployed to develop land on the Ishikari plain (Shigematsu, 1970, pp. 151–152). Due to of the rapid construction and opening of the prison, however, essential preparations were still outstanding. The prison was thus run on a rather provisional basis for the first few months (Shigematsu, 1970, p. 152). Sorachi Prison soon received an impressive number of inmates. In spite of the facility having been planned for only 1,200 individuals, in 1890 the highest number of occupants was reached with 3,048 convicts. In the same year, its staff totalled 475, with one prison warden, one vice-warden, nine secretaries, 29 head guards, 372 prison guards, six prison doctors, three errand boys, 12 assistants, and 42 lesser employees (HSY, 1993 [1892], p. 550). Members of staff often settled in the vicinity of the prison with their families. Therefore, particularly during the first period, there was a lot of interaction between the facility and its environment, and it is impossible to fathom the density of this prison complex, to which, according to Shigematsu, no present-day Japanese prison can compare (Shigematsu, 1970, p. 153).

According to the contemporary witness report of Atsumi Masao from the year 1939, the level of activity in the city of Ishikishiri was closely linked to the establishment and the closing of the prison. Especially in the first years, Sorachi Prison seemed to form the heart of the city, because at the time the prison was the only place providing medical care and premises for the operation of a school. So the arrangement was that prison doctors would treat prison members in the mornings and village people in the afternoon. The children of the prison staff were taught on the premises until the first school was constructed in 1886. In addition, Ishikishiri was for a time the only place in Sorachi-*gun* and Yubari-*gun* with a post office and a hospital – which contributed considerably to the important regional role of the city at the time (Atsumi, as cited in Nasu, 1987, p. 34). Also remarkable are prison warden Watanabe and his constant efforts to improve Ichikishiri, for example his struggle to source clean drinking water and the planting of an avenue of pines (Atsumi, quoted in Nasu, 1987, pp. 35–36).

When the prison was finally closed, Atsumi says, the city lost part of its liveliness. It becomes clear that, at least in the eyes of this particular witness, Sorachi Prison was far more than just a space to house convicts. It had enabled the city to develop and provided its inhabitants with jobs, education and medical care. This aspect is very important and symptomatic of the role the prisons of Hokkaido had within their wider surroundings before 1886.

In comparison with Kabato Prison, the spatial distribution as well as the organization of the Sorachi facility already possessed modern traits. Sorachi Prison was divided into three organizational sectors: the administrative department, the security department and the financial department. Its spatial structure, too, was highly functional. Directly next to the main entrance, there was an office section, which also contained utility sheds, a doctor's office and rice storage. The security department area comprised the security headquarters, kitchen, washroom, drying room (for laundry), examination room, refectory, prisoners' quarters, infirmary, solitary confinement, a dark room, the schoolroom, the miso and soy manufacture, various workshops and the guards' quarters. The entire prison was surrounded by a black fence, which had a separate gate for prisoners leaving and returning from work outside. Even after prison operations were stopped in 1901, the site was still reserved for institutional functions; and the primary school still operating in today's Mikasa was built in its place (Shigematsu, 1970, p. 153).

Industry and agriculture

Shortly after the Sorachi facility was opened, a carpentry shop, a barrel workshop and coal production were started. The reasoning may have been the need to provide the prison operations with necessary everyday objects and heating material. In 1883, a sawmill, a smithy and a tailor's workshop started operating. In addition, inmates began to pound rice in mortars and to manufacture straw goods. The same year, the use of prisoners for the rural development of the Ishikari plain started; however, unlike Kabato, no agricultural estates are mentioned in the primary sources. In 1884, the convicts finally began to produce tatami, leather and hemp products, to work in basketry and to pull cotton (HSY, 1993 [1892], p. 532). Pulling and de-dusting cotton were typical activities for inmates who had gone blind due to underground work. (Okada, as cited in Nasu, 1987, p. 26). From 1885, prisoners were also employed in a brickworks and in miso and soy sauce production. In 1886, the convicts started to produce paper, and a year later, they were also doing stonemasonry. In 1888, a match factory, a rope manufacture and a dye works were added to the existing workshops.

The work situation at Sorachi Prison changed abruptly in 1889, when 660,000 *tsubo* (approx. 2,185 sq. km) of arable land and 60,000 *tsubo* (approx. 198.6 sq. km) of virgin land were sold to a private company, after which all prisoners who had been working in agriculture were transferred to road or building construction. That same year, hemp and paper production as well as the stonemasonry workshop were closed. In 1891, match production and the use of prisoners in construction work ended, and prison operations resumed agricultural colonization tasks in the Ishikari plain (HSY, 1993 [1892], pp. 532–534). So, the prison labour force was from the start mainly used to press ahead with land development (Hosokawa, 1997b, p. 83).

Potable water for Ichikishiri

The important interactions between the Sorachi facility and the village of Ichikishiri has already been mentioned; however, I now examine another key example of the extent to which prison director Watanabe was dedicated to local causes.

Immediately after the prison was constructed, water wells were drilled at numerous sites in Ichikishiri; the lemon-yellow groundwater was soon found to be unfit for human consumption. In view of this situation, prison director Watanabe requested permission from the Ministry of the Interior in 1882 to instal water mains to provide Ichikishiri with potable water from the surrounding area. This request, however, was denied on the grounds that the necessary funding was currently not available, which meant that villagers and prisoners alike had to go on foot to either the base of Mikasa Mountain or to the Ikushunbetsu River to draw water. This meant that the daily water supply was only possible with great temporal and physical exertion. Moreover, the water quality of the river varied greatly, as the water was often clouded from rainfall, and the freezing of the river during the winter months made drawing water entirely impossible (SBEK, 1993 [1891], p. 603).

As the government failed to send specialists to Ichikishiri to solve the problem, the prison administration itself actively began to look for a suitable alternative water source. This lead to the discovery of a stream in Nuppaomanai, 2.8 kilometres east of the prison. As early as October 1882, Watanabe reported the finding to Yamada Akiyoshi of the Ministry of the Interior, who visited Sorachi to inspect and sent a secretary to review the source (SBEK, 1993 [1891], p. 603). The situation nonetheless did not change, and despite Watanabe's persistent efforts, this difficult state continued into the year 1886.

Change finally came with the establishment of the Hokkaido-chō, to which the prison director turned with his concerns in January 1886. Within four months, Iwamura Michitoshi, the first governor of the newly established Hokkaido prefecture, approved the water mains construction, which had been continuously postponed during the three-ken period. At this time, 2,832 people were already living in Ichikishiri, of whom 1,630 were inmates of Sorachi Prison (Shigematsu, 1970, p. 227).

Despite Iwamura's permission to build, the population of Ichikishiri still had to wait over two-and-a-half years to receive water from the Nuppaomanai source. In January 1888, construction work began at last, carried out entirely by Sorachi prisoners under the supervision of two technicians, and was completed by December that same year. The construction of a dam and the building of a water reservoir in Nuppaomanei for agricultural irrigation provided additional support for the local population. This made Ichikishiri the first place with such a water main in Hokkaido, and a far second after Yokohama in Japan (Shigematsu, 1970, p. 227). In July 1982, a chance discovery of similar water pipes in Tsukigata proved that such lines had also been built by prisoners from Kabato Prison, although the exact construction date is not clear (HKK, 1989, p. 21). After the establishment of Kabato and Sorachi Prisons in central Hokkaido, a third *shūjikan* was built in the east of the island.

Kushiro Prison

The plan to build a prison in the vicinity of Nemuro in eastern Hokkaido had been proposed by the Ministry of the Interior to the Kaitaku-shi on 29 June 1881, before the building of Sorachi Prison. The government maintained its plans for a prison in the east of Hokkaido and sent two Ministry of the Interior officials to the Kushiro region two years later, in December 1884, to look for a suitable location. One of these men was future prison warden Ōinoue Terusaki. The final report to the Interior Ministry emphasized the favourable location of the two villages Shibecha and Teshikaga. The only thing needed to make concrete future steps was the approval of the Governor of Nemuro Prefecture. However, this meant another potential delay: in the spring of 1885, Governor Yuchi Sadamoto called attention to the results of a survey amongst settlers showing that the Kushiro region was considered an excellent area for colonization; establishing a prison there, Yuchi feared, would discourage future settlers, and therefore the prison site should be rejected.

After that, both Ōinoue and Yuchi went to Tokyo to move the debate into the institutional framework of the Ministry of the Interior, and six months later, on 4 September 1885, it appears that an agreement was reached with the help of Interior Minister Yamagata Aritomo. The building in Shibecha (Kawakami-*gun*) was started on 21 September 1885 (Shigematsu, 1970, p. 158).

The circumstances preceding the establishment of Kushiro Prison show that the construction of central prisons in Hokkaido was by no means always a smooth process. Looking at the actions of Prefecture Governor Yuchi, it becomes clear that regional interests, such as maintaining a good reputation for recruiting settlers, did not always coincide with national interests.

Because of the short notice for construction and the insecure funding situation, the first prison building to be constructed was very poor but was expanded and improved over the years. As there was a building contract for the boiler room and the guard and prisoner quarters, these were quickly finished, while the remaining buildings were built by 300 Sorachi prisoners. The spatial structure was to be the same as Sorachi Prison's. However, internal organization at Kushiro Prison in its initial year differed from the other two prisons insofar as financial matters were handled by an Interior Ministry employee and there was an additional Department of Agriculture and Industry as well as the administrative and security departments (Hosokawa, 1997b, p. 86).

Finally, Kushiro Prison was opened on 15 November 1885, and Ōinoue Terusaki was appointed its warden. Only a few days after the prison opening, 94 convicts were transferred to Kushiro from Tokyo, Miyagi and Sorachi. They were promptly put to work on the unfinished prison buildings. Their tasks mainly consisted of felling wood, processing it into construction material and transporting it. In April the next year, the expansion of the penitentiary appeared to have progressed sufficiently to enable the prison to take charge of another 110 prisoners from Miyagi and Kabato. However, a lack of guards frustrated any further ambitions of the prison's expansion. Faced with this situation, a nationwide campaign was started to recruit more prison guards (SECH, 1993 [1891], p. 465). The relevant family registers show that the majority of the early guards came from the Kagoshima and Aomori prefectures (Shigematsu, 1970, p. 160). When high property tax led to many guards resigning their posts from 1894 to 1895, many *tondenhei* members were appointed as guards (KSKK, 1992, p. 47). Fortunately, the city of Shibecha began to record its prison history at an early date, and we therefore have contemporary witness reports from the staff of the Kushiro facility. For example, during a round table discussion about the prison on 7 July 1940, former guards gave an account of their experience. Originally from Kagoshima, Maruta Toshio was one of the 170 guards recruited by Ōinoue in October 1886. Maruta describes his journey to Shibecha as follows:

> I came to Shibecha in Meiji 19 [1886] when I was 23 years old. At the time, Hokkaido was known as Ezo, and when you said that you were going to Ezo, this meant you would never return because wolves and bears would attack you [there]. I came here from Yokohama by boat, travelling with a group of 170 others from Kagoshima. When I arrived in Kushiro, I saw mountains and hills everywhere, and I asked myself whatever had I come here for. When I looked around me, I saw houses showing underneath the snow, and was alarmed at the thought that rice would certainly not grow here, asking myself how people could eat here. At the time, there were no more than 200 households in the area of the Kushiro harbor. As we arrived at this harbor, we started out to Shibecha on foot. People told us we had to walk 12 *ri* [approx. 46.8 km, P.J.] on foot, and there was no road or anything. Then all 170 men went up the river in boats that had been waiting for us, and I was surprised when we were finally told we had arrived in Shibecha. (. . .) Then we got eight Ainu as errand boys to help us. The hair of these Ainu was so thick that it was impossible to tell whether they had eyes, and they wore a short garment reaching down to their navel that is hard to describe (. . .) I thought we would be afraid of the Ainu, but the Ainu saw us and were frightened (. . .) When we later asked [the vice-warden and a head guard, P.J.] why the Ainu were frightened when seeing us, we were answered that our Kagoshima customs were surprising, we were dressed in short garments made of dappled cotton fabric which did not cover our ankles.
>
> (Maruta, 1997, pp. 343–344)

This passage vividly describes the journey from Kagoshima to Shibecha and highlights the stereotypes associated with Hokkaido among the general Japanese population at the time. Although the name Ezo had already ceased to exist 17 years before, the place name was still in use, according to Maruta, and was associated with fantastic imaginings. We get a glimpse of the culture shock the southern Japanese recruits experienced in wintry northern Japan, which for Maruta probably climaxed in his encounter with the Ainu and the resulting unexpected perception of themselves as outsiders.

Due to the sudden increase in guard staff, the Kushiro facility had, for the short duration of a month, a rather curious ratio of guards to inmates: one inmate was matched by three to four guards. According to Maruta's report, many inmates were busy producing artisanal products and straw goods at the time, although most of them did not take to the work (Maruta, 1997, p. 344). This exceptional state soon came to an abrupt end in November 1886 with the arrival of 500 convicts from Tokyo and Miyagi. One month later, in December 1886, the convict labour deployment to Atosanupuri's Sulphur Mountain commenced.

In terms of prisoner type, Kushiro Prison was mainly reserved for former members of the military police. Thus, external security measures had to be taken, and there was even a rumour that the *tondenhei* units of the nearby town Akkeshi had received a secret order to keep the prison under additional surveillance (Shigematsu, 1985, p. 144). Probably one of the best-known Kushiro inmates is Tsuda Sanzō. Tsuda's failed attempt to take the life of Russian crown prince Nikolai II on 11 May 1891 led to him being sent first to Kabato, then transferred to Kushiro where he eventually committed suicide (Shigematsu, 1970, pp. 163–164).

In addition to the different tasks of the prison-owned manufactures, the Kushiro inmates were also used in land development. By the time the prison was shut in 1901, they had cleared more than 218.24 hectares of land (Higashi, 1997, p. 310). In contrast to Kabato and Sorachi, Kushiro Prison experimented with wet rice cultivation starting in 1891, and actually achieved modest results (Higashi, 1997, p. 310). The successful application of American agricultural methods is another peculiarity of the Kushiro facility (Shigematsu, 1985, p. 144). Because of these agricultural activities, the local population viewed Kushiro Prison as an experimental station for agricultural practices (Misu, 1994, p. 36).

Notes

1 Different sources mention different place names. While a printed source from 1891 names the place as "Tōsunai", Higashi cites the town of "Tōmunai". In both texts, the name is written using the *katakana* syllabary (Higashi, 1997, p. 310).

2 This organization was founded in Niigata under the leadership of Ōhashi Ichizō, and aimed to act as an agent for farmers from Niigata to become settlers in Hokkaido (Higashi, 1997, p. 334). After unsuccessful attempts at colonizing the village of Horomui (Sorachi-*gun*), the organization bought the land reclaimed by the forced labour. Initially, it attempted to establish a large-scale agricultural operation on this land, but soon had to give up this mode of production for more successful, smaller units (Enomoto, 1999, p. 274).

Bibliography

Botsman, D.V. 2005, *Punishment and Power in the Making of Modern Japan*. Princeton and Oxford: Princeton University Press.

Enomoto, M. 1999, *Hokkaido no rekishi*. Sapporo: Hokkaido shinbunsha.

Foucault, M. 1991, *Discipline and Punish*. *The Birth of the Prison*. London: Penguin.

Fujii, F. 1997, Hokkaido shūjikan ni okeru tōsō no kenkyū. In Takashio, H. and Nakayama, K. eds. *Hokkaido shūjikan ronkō*. Tokyo: Kōbundō, pp. 91–147.

Goffman, E. 1991, *Asylums*. *Essays on the Social Situation of Mental Patients and other Inmates*. London: Penguin.

Higashi, K. 1997, Kaitakushi jōno Hokkaido shūjikangoku. In Takashio, H. and Nakayama, K. eds. *Hokkaido shūjikan ronkō*. Tokyo: Kōbundō, pp. 293–338.

Hokkaidō kaitaku kinenkan. ed. 1989, *Shūjikan. Kaitaku to shūjin rōdō*. Sapporo: Hokkaidō kaitaku kinenkan.

Hosokawa, K. 1997a, Meiji zenki no Hokkaido shūjikan. In Takashio, H. and Nakayama, K. eds. *Hokkaido shūjikan ronkō*. Tokyo: Kōbundō, pp. 59–74.

Hosokawa, K. 1997b, Meiji zenki no Hokkaido shūjikan zoku kō. In Takashio, H. and Nakayama, K. eds. *Hokkaido shūjikan ronkō*. Tokyo: Kōbundō, pp. 75–90.

HSY= *Hokkaido shūjikan yōran*, 1993 [1892]. In ASHK = Asahikawa shishi henshū kaigi. ed. 6. *Shūjikan (kangokuho) shiryō*. Asahikawa: Asahikawa shishi henshū kai-gi, pp. 518–553.

Koike, Y. 1981 [¹1973], *Kusaritsuka: Jiyūminken to shūjin rōdō no kiroku*. Tokyo: Gendaishi shuppankai.

KSER= *Kabato shūjikan enkaku ryakki*. 1993 [1891]. In ASHK = Asahikawa shishi henshū kaigi. ed. 6. *Shūjikan (kangokuho) shiryō*. Asahikawa: Asahikawa shishi henshū kai-gi, pp. 504–518.

KSKK = Kushiro shūjikan wo kataru kai. ed. 1992, *Kushiro shūjikan ni kinmu shita hitobito*. Kushiro: Kushiro shūjin wo kataru kai (= Kushi-ro shūjikan no kiroku; 5).

Maruta, Y. 1997, Kushiro shūjikan wo shinobu zadankai. In Takashio, H. and Nakayama, K. eds. *Hokkaido shūjikan ronkō*. Tokyo: Kōbundō, pp. 339–367.

Misu, T. 1994, *Kushiro shūjikan*. Kushiro: Misu Tatsuo.

Nagai, H. and Ōba, Y. eds. 1999, *Hokkaido no hyakunen*. Tokyo: Yamakawa shuppansha (= Kenmin hyakunenshi; 1).

Nasu, K. 1987, *Sorachi shūjikan no shokuseikatsu*. Iwamizawa: Hokkaido shinbunsha.

SBEK= *Sorachi bunkan enkaku ki*. 1993 [1891]. In ASHK = Asahikawa shishi henshū kaigi. ed. 6. *Shūjikan (kangokuho) shiryō*. Asahikawa: Asahikawa shishi henshū kai-gi, pp. 553–627.

SECH= *Shūjikan enkaku chō* 1993 [1891]. In ASHK = Asahikawa shishi henshū kaigi. ed. 6. *Shūjikan (kangokuho) shiryō*. Asahikawa: Asahikawa shishi henshū kai-gi, pp. 349–404.

Shigematsu, K. 1970, *Hokkaido gyō keishi*. Tokyo: Zufu shuppan.

Shigematsu, K. 1985, *Zukan Nihon no kangokushi*. Tokyo: Yūzankaku shuppan.

Yamada, Y. 1997, Hokkaido shūjikan shi. In Takashio, H. and Nakayama, K. eds. *Hokkaido shūjikan ronkō*. Tokyo: Kōbundō, pp. 167–291.

4 Hard labour as penal servitude, 1886–1894

While rural development advanced slowly during the previously mentioned three-*ken* government (1881–1885), and the labour assignments of prison inmates were carried out quite moderately, this was to change abruptly in the year 1886.

This chapter documents the day labour of convicts working in sulphur and coal mines, in extensive road and building construction, and in the expansion of waterways. All this work served the Japanese colonial regime in Hokkaido. Linked to this are two other prisons in Abashiri and Tokachi. This chapter concludes by explaining why external prison labour was discontinued in 1894.

Formulating a prison labour policy

The proposal to abolish the three-*ken* government and establish the Hokkaido-chō was enacted on 26 January 1886. The reasons for this change were the Meiji government's suspicion of the three-*ken* government's efficiency. As a consequence, prime minister Itō Hirobumi sent government official Kaneko Kentarō to Hokkaido to inspect the region. Kaneko had studied law at Harvard University in his younger years and was expected to contribute significantly to the development of a new administrative and colonization concept for the north island (Shigematsu, 1970, p. 173). The scholar travelled throughout Hokkaido for more than two months, and upon his return to Tokyo in early October 1886, he presented a final report on his observations of the island's shortcomings along with suggestions for their rectification. A crucial point of this report was the call to abolish the three-*ken* government in no uncertain terms and to establish a central administration in its place (Enomoto, 1999, p. 254). Kaneko's report also included statements regarding the future role of the three central prisons in light of the dire labour shortages on Hokkaido. This very important passage is quoted here in full:

On the use of convicts in road construction: Road routes have already been determined and fully surveyed, and as soon as the budget structure for the costs of rural development has been announced, it will be necessary to begin work quickly. On initiating rural development: As least 10 *ri* [app. 40 km, P.J.] or more of densely forested area must be felled along the route, dark mountain ridges flattened, and water conduits dug into the valleys. If common labourers are hired for these extremely arduous tasks and are unable to bear the workload, we will be in a situation where wages will rise to a very high level. For this reason, prisoners from the prefectures of Sapporo and Nemuro should be relocated and deployed here. These are rough hoodlums by nature, and if they are unable to bear the work and are broken by it, then the situation is no different than that of common labourers, who leave behind wives and children, and whose remains must be interred in the ground. And furthermore, if – as is the case today – there are a great number of hardened criminals and the steadily rising cost of imprisonment must be financed by the government, then these convicts should be put to work in these important sectors. If they are unable to bear it and perish then it is, in light of today's situation, in which reports are made on the extreme difficulty of funding prisons, to be considered a politically strategic reduction of these persons that can take place in no other way. Furthermore, if we are to compare the wages of a common labourer with that of a prisoner, we see that the daily wage of labourers in Hokkaido is no less than 40 *zeni*, while prisoners receive no more than 18 *zeni* per day. In the case that prison labour is used, a great portion of the cost of development would be saved in comparison to the use of common labourers. This I call killing two birds with one stone!

Today, dangerous criminals with more than 10 years of incarceration are sent to Hokkaido, where they are given accommodation, clothing and food, all things that must be imported from central Japan at an extraordinarily high cost. The work methods are no different than those of minor criminals. This preferential treatment and waiting for the day of repentance, upon which the intention is to turn them into residents, not only hinders how these hardened criminals are disciplined, it is also disadvantageous for the government. Therefore, I ask that such convicts are gathered and put to such arduous tasks that common labourers cannot bear.

(Kaneko, as cited in Shigematsu, 1970, p. 174)

Three main points can be gleaned from this passage: death as an economic calculation factor; price comparisons between free and prison labour forces; and possible criticism of Itō's 1880 ideas on the socio-economic benefit of sending prisoners to Hokkaido.

Apparently fully aware that the construction of roads would cause extreme exertion and bring about numerous casualties, Kaneko suggests mobilizing convicts instead of employing "free" workers for the project. He first argues his point about social savings before mentioning the actual financial economies to be gained: in contrast to common labourers, convicts would not leave behind wives and children, and therefore their remains would not need to be buried. According to this reasoning, the death of prisoners seemed more justifiable than that of other citizens and would even reduce economic pressure on the prisons. As we have seen, however, many prisoners actually had families. The example of Nakano Jirosaburō and his wife Ito – mentioned in Chapter 2 – illustrates how families adapted to the imprisonment of a spouse and father. Prison directors like Watanabe Koreaki in Sorachi even helped families to cope with the situation. Kaneko was therefore wrong when suggesting that prisoners had no family members. By denying the convicts family membership and any right to a proper burial, he also, in a way, refutes their existence as social beings and unashamedly ascribes them with the characteristics of a commodity.

In the second part of Kaneko's text, the wages of convicts and free labourers are compared. The cynically low remuneration of the convicts, however, cannot be understood as a lesson in teaching civic values. While this notion – the rehabilitation of common convicts into honest citizens – was still a component of Itō's reasoning in 1879, Kaneko passes over this function of prison labour entirely, reducing it solely to its economic value.

Beyond this, it also seems that Kaneko criticizes the ideas of his contemporary Itō and the prisons' previous accomplishments in manufacturing and agriculture as representing "favouritism" (*yūtai*). Disregarding the successful efforts to establish subsistence farming and to produce their own everyday items and clothing, Kaneko characterizes the Hokkaido inmates as parasites who neither contributed to their own sustenance nor were of any use to the state. He derides the opinion that it was possible to rehabilitate inmates to become law-abiding citizens, and finally calls for an intensification of their work duties. Kaneko likely learned the strategy of using convicts for hard labour and thus counteracting labour shortages from his brother-in-law Dan Takuma, the future managing director of the Mitsui Corporation. After studying in the US, Dan ran the coal mine in Miike (Fukuoka) from 1884, which had been using forced labourers since 1873 (Koike, 1981, pp. 102–103).

Importantly, there was a great difference between Kaneko's reasoning and that of his two less influential contemporaries Itō Hirobumi and Yamagata Aritomo. In 1879, Itō's ultimate intention was to rehabilitate the convicted individuals through labour, and then settle them in Hokkaido after their release. Yamagata declared his support for the intensification of prison labour, yet he also expressed his hope to thus prevent repeated delinquency.[1] Itō and Yamagata have in common at least a tendency towards humane thinking, which appears to be entirely absent from Kaneko's commentary (Koike, 1981, p. 103).

Thus, prison labour was intensified in order to accelerate the rural development of Hokkaido. The expansion of the road network in the north of the island turned into a colonization priority. Three roads needed to be built: one joining Sapporo with Sorachi, Kamikawa, Kushiro and Nemuro; another from Kabato heading north to Mashike; and a third from Kushiro to Abashiri (Shigematsu, 1970, p. 186). The inmates of the prisons in Sorachi, Kabato and Kushiro – now all under the authority of the Hokkaido-chō – were to be the main labour force for the realization of these development plans. Thus, in the years to follow, the expansion of the highway network was one of the Hokkaido prisoners' main activities.

The daily prison routine

Starting in the year 1889, daily routines in Japanese prisons were standardized by the so-called *Kangokusoku shikō kisoku* (Prison Regulatory Statutes). This section describes the daily living and working conditions of the prisoners using the standard schedule used in prisons on Hokkaido.

The daily schedule was subject to seasonal changes, especially as most of the prison labour assignments took place outdoors and were thus dependent on the availability of daylight. It should also be noted that it was not possible to easily apply the original schedule, intended to be used for the whole of the country, in Hokkaido's extreme climatic conditions (HSY, 1993[1892], p. 533).

The prisoners' wake-up call was likely shortly before sunrise. For breakfast, there was basically miso soup and rice, prepared by a chef and served to the prisoners by aides along with mess gear. When the command to eat was given by the guards, the inmates had five to seven minutes to hastily consume their breakfast before the next command brought an end to the meal (Nasu, 1987, p. 94). In a newspaper article from the *Hokkaido mainichi shinbun* dated 23 March 1892, prison mealtimes were described as follows:

At mealtimes, the guard gives the command and His Majesty the Emperor is solemnly thanked for his holy goodness in giving this gift of food. As soon as these thanks are said, as if from one mouth, the eating begins, and a thunderous noise sets in, almost enough to make one deaf. As soon as the chopsticks are in hand, a guard appears at side and with the words, "Go, go. Eat fast!!" The whole thing goes so quickly, that the meal is over in five minutes, and in slow cases seven.

If anybody is left who has not finished by then, they are given a severe criticism, and there are also some who are handed out a beating.

(*Hokkaido mainichi shinbun* 23 March 1892,
as cited in Nasu, 1987, p. 94)

In terms of meal portions, the 1889 prison regulations detailed a specific amount of rice and grain, measured in *gō* (0.18 litres), with a meal consisting of four parts unpolished rice and six parts millet (HKK, 1989, p. 23). From this list, it is possible to discern the following groups and their daily rations: heavy labourers (1.44–1.26 litres); light labourers (1.08–0.9 litres); the ill and unoccupied (0.918–0.9 litres); those punished by food reduction (0.63–0.32 litres); and the seriously ill (0.54–0.216 litres) (HKK, 1989, p. 24). A variety of vegetables were served as side dishes, with vegetables also being used as a reward or distributed as a night-time snack (Nasu, 1987, p. 66).

Work usually started immediately after breakfast, with a work shift before lunchtime ranging from 4 hours and 20 minutes to 7 hours, depending on the season. The lunch break was extremely short and meals were presumably taken directly at the work site. Unfortunately, the table provides no information on the time of dinner.

The 1889 prison regulations stipulated a khaki-coloured work uniform for convicts, which had the purpose of making escaped convicts immediately recognizable. A report in the *Hokkaido mainichi shinbun* on 29 November 1888 recounts that khaki-coloured clothing thereafter triggered alarmed reactions among the local populations. According to the article, a certain Sandaban Tarō was identified as being suspicious because he wore khaki-coloured *tabi* (socks) in the port town of Otaru. He was assumed to be an escaped convict and was turned into the police, being released only after his origins were verified. The article concludes with a proposal to discontinue the sale of khaki-coloured *tabi* in order to prevent such confusion in the future (*Hokkaido mainichi shinbun* 29 November 1888, as cited in Kuwabara, 1982, pp. 177–178). In addition to the recognizable uniforms, the convicts' heads were shaved in a kind of tonsure, likewise intended to enable immediate detection (Kuwabara, 1982, p. 174). While working outside the prison facilities, convicts were put in shackles and supervised by guards armed with pistols and swords on horseback (Nasu, 1987, p. 95). These practices aimed to limit prisoners' attempts to escape.

The hours after putting down one's daily work and returning to prison were, in accordance with prison regulations, reserved for religious morality lessons, which were held in a separate classroom on Sundays and days off (KSKK, 1994, p. 7). Prison chaplains usually gave these morality lessons. In Sorachi Prison well-educated prisoners also taught illiterate prisoners how to read. The moral virtues of some of the imprisoned members of the Freedom

and People's Rights Movement were even considered psychologically supportive for others (Shigematsu, 1970, pp. 226–228). It should be noted that
gambling was practiced in the prisons from the very beginning, despite the
threat of punishment (Yamada, 1997, p. 207); some of the prisoners' playing
cards, with floral motifs, exist in archives today (HKK, 1989, p. 28).

The Horonai coal mines

As early as 1873, an American engineer in the service of the Kaitaku-shi,
Benjamin Smith Lyman, discovered coal deposits in Horonai. He reported
on the large quantities, high quality and favourable stratification of this coal,
and recommended exploitation of the coalfield (Heltmann, 1996, p. 30). The
Kaitaku-shi were subsequently allocated funds in the amount of 1.5 mil-
lion yen by the government in 1878 for developing the mining industry in
Horonai and for rehabilitating the mines in Kayanuma (Enomoto, 1999,
p. 215). As for labour, Kuroda first tried to force the Ainu from Sakhalin to
work in the mines by ordering their forced resettlement from Sōya to the
region of Ishikari. This, however, provoked protests from a judge named
Matsumoto Jūrō, who saw similarities between mining operations and the
conditions in the penal colonies of Sado and Shiranuku (Shigematsu, 1970,
pp. 151–152). Although the Ainu were released from the obligation to work
in the coal mines, they had to serve the rural development of Hokkaidō in
other ways. The Sakhalin Ainu deported to the Ishikari plain were forced
to work in agriculture in the region, in spite of the judge's protests, who
then resigned from office. The Ainu, accustomed to fishing and the northern
climate, served as forced farmers over the next years, many of them becoming casualties of cholera due to their changed way of life. Most Ainu were
unable to return home to Sakhalin until after the Russo-Japanese War of
1905 (Enomoto, 1999, p. 211; Shigematsu, 1970, p. 152).

Because the Ainu were no longer considered a potential labour force for
the coal mines of Horonai and because the recruitment of ordinary coal
miners proved difficult, it was decided by the government in 1881 to use
prison labourers in the mines. According to historian Koike Yoshitaka, the
government's decision also explains the way the construction of the prisons
was pushed through, as the mines needed to supplement their workforce
with convicts (Koike, 1981, p. 100). A prompt deployment of prisoners to
Horonai failed, however, due to the lack of necessary infrastructure such
as barracks near the coalfield. On 15 August 1882, Sorachi Prison warden
Watanabe turned to the Ministry of the Interior and explained the adverse
situation:

> Although the distance is only about 10 *chō* [approx. 327 m, P.J.], the
> effort and time – about four hours – needed to cover the distance from

the prison [to the coalfield, P.J.] every day on extremely difficult roads is very troublesome. The heavy snow in winter is also very unfavorable for outdoor work assignments.

(Watanabe, as cited in SBEK, 1993 [1891], p. 566)

However, the government refused to fund the construction of the barracks and left it to Watanabe to solve the problem. The latter left for Sapporo and borrowed a sum of 3,400 yen from the authority responsible for the coalfields (which was at the time subordinate to the Ministry of Infrastructure), planning to repay it in monthly instalments with the profits made from the prisoners' labour (Shigematsu, 1970, p. 152). Finally, in July 1883, 60 prisoners began work in the coal mines, a year after Sorachi Prison opened. The number of prison labourers increased steadily, and in November of that same year, the prison labour force had grown to around 250 men (Nakamura, 1998, p. 59). In contrast to the work in agriculture or in workshops previously discussed, the prisoners chosen for this hard underground labour were mainly long-term prisoners (sentences of more than 12 years) with a powerful build aged 20–40 years old (HKK, 1989, p. 15).

Despite the physical fitness of the chosen prisoners, their coal production was so low (HKK, 1989, p. 15) that ordinary coal miners were also recruited to Horonai, their numbers proportionally decreasing compared to the prisoners over the years. In 1885, the total workforce included 63 per cent of ordinary workers, while a year later, 55 per cent of workers were convicts. When the administration of the Horonai coal mines was transferred to the Sorachi Prison management in 1887, the proportion of prison labourers again rose to 74 per cent, and to 78 per cent in 1888 (Mizuno, quoted in Nakamura, 1998, p. 59).

So, the pace of the coal mining was increasing dramatically, which advanced Horonai to the position of the nation's third most prolific coal mine, after Miike and Takashima. Domestically, the Mitsui Corporation was the largest buyer of this coal, but exports to Hong Kong and Singapore were also on the rise (Enomoto, 1999, p. 260). Production costs were kept low through the use of forced labour, enabling the Mitsui Corporation to deliver the cheapest possible coal to the Asian markets (Botsman, 2005, p. 185).

The working conditions in the mines were extremely hard. Work was carried out in two shifts of 12 hours, with the day and night shifts exchanging each week. For those who were occupied in transportation and processing, the workday began at 5 a.m. and – punctuated only by a short lunch break – continued until 4 p.m. Inside the mine, the corridors were so tight that the convicts could only move about by crawling on their bellies and had to work lying down. The air must have been very bad during the day. Especially dangerous were the airborne flammable gases and the ubiquitous coal dust. The wearing of the prison work uniform was also an unpleasant affair; the clothing was often soaked with rain and sweat and did not dry until the next day. The prisoners nonetheless had to wear the clothing, even once they had started to smell as badly as fish oil (Mikasa-shi, as cited in Kuwabara, 1982, p. 172).

These conditions greatly affected the workers' health. In 1889, 663 of the 1,966 prisoners in Horonai were injured and 13 died (HKK, 1989, p. 16), tragedies which could be attributed to the harmful polluted air, gas explosions and the abysmal quality of the drinking water.

In the summer of 1893, Okada Asajirō, a medical doctor from Tokyo University, inspected the mine and reported the following:

> Meals are not regulated, with workers eating and drinking at will. The foul and putrid drinking water is unfit for human consumption. For this reason, the prisoners fall ill from digestive diseases, chronic stomach problems, and diarrhea. (. . .) There is no separation between the latrines and the places where meals are eaten, and the prisoners breathe dust and bad air polluted by coal dust and gases.
>
> (Okada, as cited in Nasu, 1987, pp. 25–26)

During his visit to the Sorachi facility, Okada also noticed the great number of crippled and blind inmates, dramatically stating: "He who enters this mine, an inimical danger equal to a tragic and gruesome arrow, advances into the kingdom of death" (Okada, as cited in Nasu, 1987, p. 26).

It was not only these health threats that the doctor took issue with, but also the "deplorable" habits of the prisoners themselves. Firstly, the job site provided ample opportunities to attempt escape despite constant surveillance, and secondly, some prisoners were able to eat better food than they were thought to deserve. This was made possible by trade and exchange with "free" workers, despite it being forbidden. Thirdly, prisoners secretly brewed sake in the mines by saving leftover rice and allowing it to ferment in the caves (Okada, as cited in Nasu, 1987, pp. 26–27). Okada's telling report ends with the urgent recommendation to cease the employment of prison labourers in the Horonai mines.

Due to the Sino-Japanese War, however, coal production in Horonai rose again in the year 1894, with a total of 18,979 tonnes being mined and mostly shipped abroad. Despite this support for the national war efforts, the Japanese mass media increasingly reported on the senseless use of prisoners in the Horonai mines and on their victims. As a consequence, the Meiji government initiated in December 1894 the process of ending prison labour in Horonai (Shigematsu, 1970, p. 226). In 1913 the management of the mines was eventually transferred to the Mitsui Corporation (Culter, 1999, p. 37).

It can be estimated that between 1883 and 1891, 81 prison labourers died and 3,301 were injured while working in the Horonai mines. According to notes in the primary sources, more than half of those injured also suffered from eye diseases (SECH, 1993 [1891], p. 443). Together with the forced labourers in Miike and Takashima, the Horonai convicts significantly supported the launch of the coal industry, which was Japan's only energy industry at the time (Nakamura, 1998, p. 60) and essential to the nation's industrialization and militarization.

The sulphur mountain in Atosanupuri

In Hokkaido, the region around lake Kussharo was known for its wealth of sulphur. The Ainu knew about the sulphur mountain in Atosanupuri because of the white, strange smelling smoke that came out of it. Maps of Ezo's Matsumae han indicated the sulphur mountain with the name *tsuru take* (crane summit) (Shigematsu, 1970, p. 232).

In 1885, Yamada Sakurō, a banker from Hakodate, became responsible for the administration of the Sulphur Mountain. In order to ensure the smooth operation of sulphur extraction, transportation of the raw material and construction of a refinery, Yamada turned to the founder of the Yasuda-zaibatsu Yasuda Zenjirō, a resident of Hakodate, to ask for a loan. The year before, Yasuda himself had ordered research to be conducted on the sulphur mountains in the region and supported Yamada, fully aware that the Atosanupuri mine was a treasure trove worth investing in (Koike, 1981, p. 107).

In order to increase the number of workers while still keeping costs low, Yamada signed a contract the following year, in 1886, with Ōinoue, the director of the newly opened Kushiro Prison. The contract obligated the prison administration to supply the company with around 500 prison labourers for a daily wage of 15 *sen* for a duration of 10 years. By comparison, the prisoners earned more in road construction, with a daily wage of 18 *sen* (Shigematsu, 1970, p. 233). A special prison yard was built near the Sulphur Mountain to house the convicts, thus avoiding the inconvenience of transporting prisoners and guards daily between the penitentiary and the work site. In December of that same year, the first convicts began working in Atosanupuri (Misu, 1994, p. 42).

The business acumen of the banker Yasuda, however, was only mildly successful. The expected profits failed to roll in and the operation of the sulphur mine was transferred to Yasuda in 1877. Supported by Iwamura and thus the Hokkaido-chō, Yasuda invested in the modernization of the sulphur operations and, in order to guarantee a profit, counted on the cheapest possible prison labour (Koike, 1981, p. 108).

With the acceleration of the raw material transport in mind, the businessman's first step was to order the construction of a local railway joining Atosanupuri with the refinery in Shibecha, built by the same company which owned the mine, to replace the previous method of transportation by sled (Koike, 1981, p. 110). Although the railway's primary purpose was goods transport, it was also available to the general population as a means of transportation. In the refinery itself, around 550 Kushiro inmates laboured alongside about 200 "free" workers (Koike, 1981, p. 109).

Prison labourers widened the Kushiro River channel for the shipping of processed material from Shibecha to Kushiro Harbour via steamboat. The convicts also installed telephone lines and built a 40-kilometre road between Shibecha and Kushiro (Koike, 1981, p. 108; Shigematsu, 1970, p. 233). At the harbour, the goods were sold to the partner company Middleton and exported to the US, Canada, Australia and China. Sulphur was an important raw material at the time, used to manufacture gunpowder and matches and to vulcanize rubber. The sulphur from Kushiro was considered worldwide as the best quality and had an excellent reputation. The city of Kushiro blossomed along with the rise of the industry (Botsman, 1999, p. 343; Koike, 1981, p. 109). Yasuda's success can be measured by looking at the sulphur output, which increased tremendously in only 2 years: while the sulphur production was at 16,000 *koku* (2,280 t) in 1886, it had risen to 58,000 *koku* (10,440 t) by 1887, and surged in 1888–177,000 *koku* (31,860 t) (Koike, 1981, p. 109).

However, Yasuda's success came at a high cost to human life. Only half a year after his company took over operation of the sulphur mine, in June 1887, half of the prisoners working there suffered from dropsy caused by undernourishment, from which 30 of them died. By this time, a total of 42 prisoners had already died. There was not a single prisoner or guard who was not affected by sulphur gas and particles in some way or another. Many inmates became blind in both eyes. A prisoner would often simply collapse from lack of nourishment or exhaustion, only to be given a "*coup de grâce*" by the sword of an especially cruel guard, put down like an animal. Such incidents were cloaked in euphemisms such as "accidental death by fall" or "death due to an escape attempt" (Shigematsu, 1970, p. 233).

The conditions suffered by the prison labourers in Atosanupuri started to improve in 1888 after a site visit by Christian prison minister Hara Taneaki. Hara was the leader of a small, dedicated group of Christians who had already made headway on prison reform in Kansai. Accompanying a group of Kobe prisoners to Kushiro in 1888, he also visited the sulphur mine. He was deeply shocked by the conditions and advised the Christian prison director Ōinoue to immediately cease the employment of convicts. Apparently moved by the words of the minister, Ōinoue contacted Yasuda about a premature cancellation of their contract (Botsman, 1999, pp. 358–359). Secondary literature does not allow us to ascertain with any surety the motives that lay behind Yasuda's agreement to this proposal. The only thing which can be stated with any certainty is that the local population was not entirely unaware of the prevailing working conditions, and that Yasuda surely wished to bring an end to certain damaging rumours about his operation by ceasing to employ prisoners (Shigematsu, 1970, p. 238).

In December 1888, prison labour employment in Atosanupuri was ultimately brought to an end. Instead, prisoners were henceforth employed mainly in bridge, road and building construction. The Kushiro prison labourers erected a total of 13 bridges. In road construction, the 42.9-kilometre-long connection between Shibecha and Akkeshi was finished by the end of December 1889, and in November of the following year a 38.5-kilometre-long road between Atosanupuri and Abashiri was completed (HKK, 1989, p. 10). Between December 1888 and May 1889, the Kushiro inmates also erected 440 buildings in the village of Ōtsu for the Akkeshi *tondenhei* (HSY, 1993 [1892], p. 536).

As for Ōinoue and Hara, at Ōinoue's request, Hara moved to Kushiro together with his family to work there as the first Christian prison chaplain. In the following years, the two were able to introduce Christian catechesis as an educational programme in all of Hokkaido's central prisons. Hara and Ōinoue's efforts certainly effected a slow improvement of Hokkado's prison conditions (Botsman, 1999, p. 59). Nevertheless, the exploitation of convict labour for colonial projects continued and intensified with the development of Hokkaido's northeast.

Colonizing the northeast

Abashiri Prison

In March 1890, Ōinoue, director of Kushiro Prison, was given an order from the Hokkaido-chō for the inmates of his facility to help build a central highway, which Sorachi Prison labourers had been working on since June 1889 (Shigematsu, 1970, p. 245). This was an approximately 235-kilometre-long road joining Abashiri with Chūbetsubuto (what is today Asahikawa) (Ōe, 1952, p. 1) which would ensure both the rural development of the region and the settlement of a military presence in northeastern Hokkaido (ASKSKK, 1992, p. 105).

Logistically, this project could only be executed with difficulty from Shibecha. So Ōinoue began looking for a suitable site for an outpost along the coast of the Sea of Okhotsk, in order to tackle the tremendous task from there. He chose the village of Kitami (today Abashiri) in the Abashiri-*gun*.

As early as April 1890 the first contingent, consisting of a head guard, guards, and 50 prisoners, began construction on the camp. After two months, construction had progressed far enough that another 50 prisoners could be housed there, with another 1,100 convicts being moved to Abashiri over the course of that year. The service buildings, however, were not completed until June 1891 (Ōe, 1952, pp. 1–2).

The large number of inmates is a first indication that the construction project was not merely that of a temporary camp for road-building purposes. Instead, it was clear from the very beginning that a prison would be built here for two reasons. Firstly, in 1890 there was a total of 7,200 convicts housed in the prisons of Hokkaido: 1,700 in Kabato, 1,200 each in Sorachi and Kushiro, with another 3,100 convicts living in barracks in camps set up to serve work sites located too far from the prisons. Although there was no reason to fear for the capacities of the various facilities, the construction of a fourth prison would prevent any possible difficulties in the case that some or all external work projects were halted. A second reason to build a fourth prison was that the Kitami region had fertile ground and weather conditions favourable for agriculture. These two factors made it possible for the future facility to operate a self-sustaining subsistence economy (Ōe, 1952, pp. 1–2).

The village of Kitami had a population of about 600 in 1890. Keeping in mind that, in that year, over 2,000 people including prisoners, staff and their families moved to Kitami (Yamaya, 1982, p. 45), it is easy to imagine that this massive influx of people brought fundamental changes to the village community. According to an unnamed contemporary witness, villagers were informed of the decision to erect a prison by a postal worker. He assured the confused citizens that there was no reason to be upset, as this was a decision made by the government. The settlers were then called upon to dedicate themselves with renewed vigour to fishing and growing vegetable crops, as the future facility would surely have a great demand to purchase such products in its early days (N. N., as cited in Yamaya, 1982, p. 46). The subsequent introduction of commercial agriculture meant great changes to daily life for the previously self-sufficient farmers.

In addition, the springing up of many new types of facilities such as *ryokan* (travel accommodations), inns and various shops changed the face of the village. These new conditions also led to higher wages. In his 1890 travel report Hokkaido-chō official Kōno Kōkichi wrote:

> While the daily wages of a day labourer were once 30 zeni, now they have risen to 50 zeni, and carpentry-related professions that once earned 50 zeni are now worth 80 zeni. Although the price of rice has

also risen, there is nobody to be found complaining about the difficulties of making a living.

(Kōno, as cited in Yamaya, 1982, p. 47)

The opening of a branch of the Nihon Bank in the area can also be traced back to the needs of the prison operations (Yamaya, 1982, p. 25). Together with the market economy, however, fear also marched into Kitami. The locals worried about prisoners' potential escape attempts. As soon as an escape was announced, few villagers dared to leave their homes. The saying, "A prisoner on the run is more terrible than a bear", demonstrates the local population's fearful attitude (Yamaya, 1982, p. 48). However, it wasn't so much the prisoners themselves as people's imaginative ideas about them that made life for the villagers more difficult. In fact, compared to the prison escape numbers of the other three prisons, there were far fewer escape attempts from Abashiri Prison. In 1891, two Abashiri prisoners tried to escape, compared with 31 in Kabato, 35 in Kushiro and as many as 68 in Sorachi. In 1892, Abashiri again took last place with four escape attempts, behind Kabato with seven, Kushiro with 28, and Sorachi with 22 (Fujii, 1997, p. 96).

In 1890, before the official opening of the prison, inmates were used for various infrastructure projects around the village. As all goods and food for the new facility had to be transported via steamboat, the convicts rebuilt Abashiri Bridge to accommodate the passage of such vessels. They also built a road joining the prison with the village of Kitami. From the very beginning, a group of prisoners were occupied in working in a match factory. The owner of this factory was Yamada Sakurō, who had shortly been the manager of the Atosanupuri mine discussed earlier. And finally, the villagers themselves could also pay for the inmates' labour (Yamaya, 1982, p. 22).

The Abashiri facility was managed by the Kushiro Prison and had the official name *Kushiro shūjikan Abashiri bunkan* (Kushiro Central Prison – Abashiri Branch Facility). In the course of restructuring Hokkaido's prisons, Abashiri became on 16 August 1891 a branch of Kabato Prison (Ōe, 1952, p. 2). Only a few days later, on 22 August, Arima Shirosuke was transferred to the position of prison director of Abashiri Prison (Shigematsu, 1970, p. 246). At the time of taking office, Arima was only 27 years old, and although he had gathered considerable experience in prison operations as chief guard in Kushiro at Ōinoue's side since 1886, such a great career jump at such a young age was considered highly unexpected (Yamaya, 1982, p. 25). As prison director, Arima had a staff of seven head guards, 136 guards, one prison minister, five secretaries, and 24 assistants (Ōe, 1952, p. 3). At the time of the official opening of Abashiri Prison, in the summer of 1891, a majority of the prisoners had already been working for several months in harsh conditions on the construction the of the Central Highway.

Building of the Central Highway

The building of the Central (Chūō) Highway was a connection between entire regions. When finished, the highway was meant to join Abashiri with Sapporo, right through central Hokkaido (Koike, 1981, p. 74). In 1889, the idea of extending the existing route up towards the north was born. Statements garnered from secondary literature on the reasons behind undertaking such a large project vary. While Shigematsu and Ōe mention only the facilitation of the settlement of northeast Hokkaido (Ōe, 1952, p. 14, Shigematsu, 1970, p. 248), Koike also emphasizes the crucial military function of the Chūō route, thereby explaining the reasons behind the pressure to complete the project within a single year (Koike, 1981, p. 74).

Although the Kurile Islands had in the 1875 Treaty of St Petersburg officially been accorded to Japan, and there was agreement about the Japanese-Russian border in Siberia, after the Crimean War in 1878 the expansion of the Trans-Siberian Railway towards the coast and the military armament at the port of Vladivostok renewed Japan's military awareness of the need to secure the borders of its northern territories (ASKSKK, 1992, p. 104). This reasoning also explains the stationing of the *tondenhei* in Hokkaido, a force that not only helped populate the region and protect the civilian settlers, but which also secured Japan's northernmost borders (Kuroda, as cited in Enomoto, 1999, p. 223). For example, Sorachi and Kabato prisoners built *tondenhei* accommodation in the two *gun*, Sorachi and Kamikawa. The Kabato inmates erected 150 buildings in the village of Takikawa from January 1888 to July 1890, and a total of 500 buildings in the village of Nagayama (today a district of what has become the city of Asahikawa) from January 1890 to December 1891, joined by the Sorachi inmates from June 1890 to May 1891 (HSY, 1993 [1892], p. 536).

Indeed, the fear of a Russian attack was reawakened in 1888 by Nagayama Takeshirō, who had once been a *tondenhei* and was now the new governor of the Hokkaido-chō. After returning from a journey to Russia, he warned the Japanese government of the acute danger from Russia and urged the settlement of the areas around Kitami and Teshio, as well as the establishment of a *tondenhei* station in the region. For these reasons, it was important to quickly extend the Ishikari road towards the north. While an average of 10 *ri* (39 km) of road had previously been built per year, Nagayama now insisted upon an extreme acceleration and a plan that would make it possible to complete 45 *ri* (175.5 km) in the same span of time (Koike, 1981, pp. 74–75).

The project was taken up from two geographical sites. As early as 29 June 1889, the first group of 37 prisoners and six supervisory staff members were sent in from Sorachi to lay the road from Chūbetsu to Kitami Pass

(HSY, 1993 [1892], p. 548). This unit was, due to the small number of work-ers, supported intermittently by employees of the private entrepreneur Satō Kurayoshi (HKK, 1989, p. 13).

In Abashiri, work began in early 1891 after the snow had melted. Of the total 1,313 inmates (SECH, 1993 [1891], p. 481), approximately 800 were selected for road construction duty and split into four units of about 200 prisoners each. Each of the four groups was led by a head guard, two super-vision assistants, and 12 guards (Ōe, 1952, p. 13). Thirty civilian construc-tion technicians were involved in the work process and about 20 Ainu were employed to supply food (Shigematsu, 1970, p. 246). The entire work group was assigned to the following fields of activity: bridge building, excavation (road construction) and barracks construction. The civilian specialists were assigned for the most part to bridge building. Carpenters among the prison-ers carried out the construction of the barracks (Koike, 1981, pp. 76–77).

The entire route was divided into 13 sections of approximately 3.5 *ri* (13.65 km) and worked on by one work group per section. After temporary overnight camps were erected in the jungle, the prison labourers went out to fell trees in a 15 *ken* (27.3 m) wide line and, using these logs, laid a road 3 *ken* (5.46 m) wide (Shigematsu, 1970, p. 246). Work did not always pro-ceed without complication. The route did not always traverse level ground, but sometimes ran through steep rocky cliffs of hard stone, marked by extremely difficult passages that could only be overcome with dynamite (Ōe, 1952, p. 14).

In order to avoid exceeding the prescribed construction period of one year, all applicable labour regulations for forced labourers were disregarded. The resulting working conditions included getting up at 3 a.m. and working until 7 p.m., with night shifts lasting until 1 a.m. (Maruta, 1997, p. 348). This tempo pushed the convicts to the brink of absolute exhaustion. A type of competition between the four work units also developed, with the leader of the fastest troop being allowed to select the next section of road to work on.

Proof of the convicts' weakened state can be found, for example, in the fact that most escapees were either immediately recaptured, or even stag-gered back into the camp, unable to survive in the wilderness with such reduced constitutions (ASKSKK, 1992, p. 101). Despite the convicts' feet being chained together in pairs, as a measure to prevent escape, getaway attempts occurred almost daily, usually ending tragically. Those captured by guards were executed with a stab of a sword or a pistol shot and per-functorily buried on the side of the road (Yamaya, 1982, p. 51). By 1982, local citizens had unearthed the remains of 60 individuals from the shallow roadside graves along the Central Highway and given them a proper burial (ASKSKK, 1992, p. 103). As most of the corpses still had iron chains on their limbs, these gravesites were dubbed *kusaritsuka* (chain mounds).

Prisoners whose lives were not ended by the hand of a guard often fell ill to one of the numerous rampant diseases. Due to the insufficient supply of food and the frequent lack of potable drinking water, a Beriberi-like form of dropsy, or edema, broke out during midsummer 1891 among all the labourers, costing the lives of a total of 156 people. Another two people died of stomach illnesses, and one inmate committed suicide (ASKSKK, 1992, p. 101).

In September 1891, the Abashiri prisoners met up in Takinoue with the Sorachi inmates, who had been working towards them from Chūbetsu. The rough work was now finished, but final improvements on the route took another three months to be completed. In early December the highway route was reported as completed according to plan (Shigematsu, 1970, p. 248).

Joined together with the 87-kilometre-long Ishikari road and the approximately 42-kilometre-long connection between Ichikishiri and Sapporo (which, incidentally, had not been built by prison labour), the Central Highway was now the first long-range highway in Hokkaido, running for a total of about 305 kilometres (Shōbunsha, 2001, pp. 5–6).

The Central Highway now linked the areas along the Ishikari, Yūbetsu and Tokoro Rivers. In anticipation of the settlement of these areas, postal stations were immediately set up along the highway to provide transportation and protection for the settlers. The establishment of *tondenhei* camps along the Kitami coast and around Tanno starting in 1892 shows that the road made it possible for immigrants to settle in the northeast of Hokkaido and was also used by the armed forces. Special manoeuvres training prepared soldiers for a Russian landing in the region. Twelve years later, the Central Highway played an important role in transporting field soldiers in the Russo-Japanese war (CDKGTHK, 1993, pp. 43–44).

A total of 292 lives were lost during the construction of this road, of which 54 were Sorachi Prison inmates and six were guards at Abashiri Prison. Of the 232 deceased Abashiri convicts, 27 died after their return to the prison of illnesses contracted while working on the road (CDKGTHK, 1993, p. 39).

Tokachi Prison

Tokachi Prison was established in the area of what is today Obihiro. Since 1883, the Banseisha settlement society had been making serious settlement efforts in the Tokachi region. This group was different from other settlement societies in that its leader, Yoda Benzō, was not of the nobility but from a farming family. The Banseisha were shaped by Yoda's idealistic visions, which were primarily rooted in making Western pioneer dreams become reality (Berque, 1980, p. 72). This could be seen, for example, in the way the group used Western agricultural methods, trying to cultivate exotic products like apples and tomatoes. The efforts of this group, however, were often stifled by frequent plagues of insects. Difficulties were compounded by a lack of infrastructure, which made it difficult to sell their produce in larger markets (Shigematsu, 1970, p. 250).

Sorachi Prison director Watanabe Koreaki had already expressed the idea of stimulating the rural development of Tokachi through prison labour in June 1889. However, at that point the plan could not be carried out for two reasons. Firstly, there was not enough funding to build a prison in Kasai-*gun*. And secondly, not enough prisoners could be spared from the Kabato, Sorachi and Kushiro facilities that year for agricultural tasks (Iida, 1997, p. 32).

In 1891, the Hokkaido-chō finally began paying closer attention to the situation of uneven rural development around Tokachi and the resulting sparse population in this region. A land-use plan for the future development of the region was set up. At the centre of this plan was Shita-Obihiro, an area settled by the Banseisha. In order to carry out this plan, 600 prisoners were moved from Abashiri and Sorachi and tasked with the development of 3,500 hectares of land around Obihiro and 100 hectares around Nukabira (Shigematsu, 1970, p. 251). Ōinoue, now the director of Kabato Prison, selected the village of Obihiro in Kasai-*gun* as the site of the future prison, and construction work began in 1893 (Iida, 1997, p. 33). While the facility was under construction, the inmates lived in temporary accommodation, with the camp retaining the name Obihiro Branch of Kushiro Prison (*Kushiro shūjikan Obihiro shutchō*) after it was finished in 1894 up until its official opening.

A total of 700 prisoners from this site worked on the last road in Hokkaido to be built by prison labour in the years from 1892 to 1894. The approximately 44-kilometre-long link between the ports of Ōtsu, Obihiro and Memuro finally made it possible to easily access the Tokachi region and ensure its connection to the rest of Hokkaido (HKK, 1989, p. 10). The prisoners also carved out the Karikachi Pass, which divided the two *kuni* Ishikari and Tokachi, with one prisoner losing his life while working. By the time Tokachi Prison was completed, the prisoners had cleared another 3,000 hectares of land for agriculture (Shigematsu, 1970, p. 251).

Tokachi Prison opened on 20 March 1895, ending its official affiliation with Kushiro Prison and becoming a branch of Kabato Prison just like Abashiri Prison. After the end of the Sino-Japanese War, in December 1895 an intensive guard recruitment campaign was started targeting the returning soldiers. This explains the great number of former military personnel among the guards of Tokachi Prison (Shigematsu, 1970, pp. 251–252).

Aside from the road construction project, the inmates of Tokachi were primarily active in agriculture. This was due to the fact that external prison labour projects had come under critical observation and commentary by this time, and in 1894 the government decided to allow such activities to phase out.

From outside to inside labour

Several developments led to a cessation of external prison labour on Hokkaido in 1894. Firstly, a number of dedicated and influential individuals campaigned for a change in convict labour use. Importantly, these localized efforts were solidly embedded in the theoretical debates and research on prisons that were taking place at the national level. Indeed, the impetus for the very first efforts towards reforming forced prison labour services on Hokkaido arose in 1888 at the initiative of the Protestant Christian prison chaplain Hara Taneaki, when he convinced Ōinoue, Kushiro Prison's director, to withdraw Kushiro inmates from the Atosanupuri sulphur mine. Ōinoue and Hara continued to push for improvements in prison conditions and managed, for example, to prevent an expansion of prison labour activities in Horonai (Botsman, 2005, pp. 191–193). In Abashiri, prison director Arima was also shocked by massive number of deaths during the construction of the Central Highway and committed himself to improving inmates' living and working conditions. Arima was not a Christian himself but respected the Protestant prison chaplains' efforts towards reforming convict labour use (Lyons, 2017, pp. 193–194).

At this time, there had been several news reports on conditions at prison labour sites. The first prison journals written by intellectual former inmates had also been published in political newspapers and magazines (Botsman, 1999, p. 357). This attracted the attention of a politically interested public to the prison debate. Academics working in the social sciences and humanities also pleaded a clear case for prison reform. For example, in 1886, the young legal scholar Ogawa Shigejirō was named Japan's first criminologist and tasked with the translation of Western crime theory texts (Botsman, 2005, p. 194). Beyond mere translation work, however, Ogawa's activities culminated in 1889 in the composition of new set of prison regulations that were intended to be a practical application of scientific principles. This "scientific basis" was in full alignment with the European spirit of the age. An example for this new spirit was the emergence of a new image of the inmate as a unique research object, whose existence should be continually studied and improved using medical and psychological controls (Botsman, 1999, pp. 364–365).

In addition to the publication of these new scientific and humane prison regulations, the 1889 arrival in Japan of German criminologist Kurt von Seebach was another key event. Functioning as an advisor to the Meiji government, von Seebach became an inspiration to prisons across the country through his criminology lectures. In his study *Kangoku sagyō ron* (Treatise on the Activities of Prisons), he pleaded for the abolition of heavy forced labour outside the prison facility and for the limitation of punishment to labour within prison grounds (Shigematsu, 1985, p. 112). Prison reforms had clearly been set in motion. Von Seebach's proposals were included during the fourth meeting of the Imperial Diet in 1892 where the authorities considered a cessation of external prison labour (HKK, 1989, p. 18).

A critical view of forced prison labour had also spread among the local population in Hokkaido. While the settlers had benefitted from peaceful exchange with the prisons during the early years of the institutions, it seemed that from 1886 onwards the use of hard convict labour had changed the views of the population towards the prisons. The fact that the villages were no longer dependent on the prisons to the same degree as during the era of the three-*ken* government may also have contributed to local criticism. A general security concern was intensified by the *Hokkaido mainichi shinbun*, which featured almost daily stories of escape attempts during the 1890s (Kuwabara, 1982, p. 173). In this way the local population's fear of the prisons was deliberately fuelled by the government as well as the media, in order to maintain their perception of political criminals as the enemy. This propaganda was sometimes so effective that there were cases of frenzied hunts for prisoners amongst the population (Kuwabara, 1982, p. 178).

In addition to the many escape attempts there were other reasons for alarm, including the fear that moral decay would arise from living in close proximity to the prisons. Specifically, people worried about the establishment of entertainment houses in the vicinity of the prisons. For example, in response to the influx of a multitude of single men working as guards at Kushiro Prison, numerous taverns and bathing houses opened in the city of Shibecha (Shibecha-chō shikō hen, as cited in Kuwabara, 1982, p. 178).

In 1894, the decision to halt all external prison labour on the island of Hokkaido was finally passed. Henceforth all prison labour tasks were limited to agriculture and activities within the prisons themselves (HKK, 1989, p. 18). A second resolution that same year is also very interesting, concerning the treatment of prisoners to be released. As previously emphasized, the reintegration of released prisoners was one of Itō Hirobumi's central arguments for the construction of prisons on Hokkaido in 1879. Since all inmates of a penitentiary served a minimum of 12 years of incarceration, the government did not contemplate the practical realization of Itō's argument for quite some time (Higashi, 1997, p. 323).

However, in 1894, the issue of the future of released prisoners took on some urgency as the incarceration period of the first cohort of inmates was coming to an end in the near future. Once again, it was the two Protestants

Ōinoue and Hara who submitted a proposal to the Hokkaido-chō to establish an Association for the Protection of Released Convicts (*menshūhogo kai*). This type of association is comparable to today's system of probation assistance. Kabato's prison minister, Tomeoka Kōsuke, rallied for the establishment of a similar institution in Tsukigata (Shigematsu, 1970, p. 266). The realization of these intentions, however, was hindered by the resistance of local communities who vehemently protested against the settlement of former criminals in Hokkaido. After numerous advisory sessions, the Hokkaido-chō had no choice but to use a trick to ensure that released convicts would disappear from the north island. The plan was to transfer prisoners to a central Japanese facility shortly before their release date. From there they could then transition into freedom. In 1894, the first group was sent to the prison in Tokyo. Then, 220 convicts arrived at Miyagi Prison, and in 1896 Tokyo Prison took in another 224 inmates from Hokkaido (Higashi, 1997, p. 323).

Itō Hirobumi's hope of settling former prisoners in Hokkaido proved to be an error of judgement. Due to the strong focus on the employment of prison labourers during the course of colonization, there were no concerted efforts made to rehabilitate them nor were the released prisoners integrated into the settler society of Hokkaido.

Note

1 Yamagata Aritomo was also still employed by the Ministry of the Interior in 1885 and gave the speech known amongst historians as *Chō kai shugi ron* (Critique of the Disciplinary Principle) after Kaneko's departure to Hokkaidō on 4 August 1885 (Shigematsu, 1970, p. 176).

Bibliography

ASKSKK = Abashiri shichō kannai sō gō kaihatsu kiseikai. ed. 1992, *Ohōtsuku he no michi. Chūō dō ro hyakunen kinen.* Tōkyō and Sapporo: Abashiri shichō kaihatsu kiseikai.

Berque, A. 1980, *La Rizière et la Banquise: Colonisation et changement culturel à Hokkaïdo.* Paris: Publications Orientalistes de France.

Botsman, D.V. 1999, *Crime, Punishment and the Making of Modern Japan, 1790–1895.* Phil. Diss., Princeton University Press.

Botsman, D.V. 2005, *Punishment and Power in the Making of Modern Japan.* Princeton and Oxford: Princeton University Press.

CDKGTHK = Chūō dōro giseisha tsuitō hikensetsu kiseikai, ed. 1993, *Rupeshipe no bohyō. Chūō dōro ni taoreta torawarebito e no chinkonfu.* Rubeshibe: Chūō dōro giseisha tsuitō hikensetsu kiseikai.

Culter, S. 1999, *Managing Decline: Japan's Coal Industry Restructuring and Community Response.* Honolulu: University of Hawaii Press.

74   *Hard labour as penal servitude, 1886–1894*

Enomoto, M. 1999, *Hokkaido no rekishi*. Sapporo: Hokkaido shinbunsha.
Fujii, F. 1997, Hokkaido shūjikan ni okeru tōsō no kenkyū. In Takashio, H. and Nakayama, K. eds. *Hokkaido shūjikan ronkō*. Tokyo: Kōbundō, pp. 91–147.
Heltmann, P.C. 1996, *Die Entwicklung des Verkehrssystems von Hokkaido*. Marburg: Japan Center of Philipps University in Marburg (= Marburger Japan-Reihe; 16).
Higashi, K. 1997, Kaitakushi jōno Hokkaido shūjikangoku. In Takashio, H. and Nakayama, K. eds. *Hokkaido shūjikan ronkō*. Tokyo: Kōbundō, pp. 293–338.
HKK = Hokkaido kaitaku kinenkan, ed. 1989, *Shūjikan. Kaitaku to shūjinrō dō*. Sapporo: Hokkaido kaitaku kinenkan.
HSY= *Hokkaido shūjikan yōran*, 1993 [1892]. In ASHK = Asahikawa shishi henshū kaigi. ed. 6. *Shūjikan (kangokuho) shiryō*. Asahikawa: Asahikawa shishi henshū kai-gi, pp. 518–553.
Iida, M. 1997, Hokkaido no ayumi to shūjikan. In Takashio, H. and Nakayama, K. eds. *Hokkaido shūjikan ronkō*. Tokyo: Kōbundō, pp. 3–41.
Koike, Y. 1981 [¹1973], *Kusaritsuka: Jiyūminken to shūjin rōdō no kiroku*. Tokyo: Gendaishi shuppankai.
KSKK = Kushiro shūjikan wo kataru kai. ed. 1994, *Kushiro shūjikan ni kinmu shita kyō goshi*. Kushiro: Kushiro shūjin wo kataru kai (= Kushiro shūjikan no kiroku; 6).
Kuwabara, M. 1982, *Kindai Hokkaido shi kenkyū josetsu*. Sapporo: Hokkaido daigaku tosho kankōkai.
Lyons, A.J. 2017, *Karma and Punishment: Prison Chaplaincy in Japan from the Meiji Period to the Present*. Phil. Diss., Harvard University Press.
Maruta, Y. 1997, Kushiro shūjikan wo shinobu zadankai. In Takashio, H. and Nakayama, K. eds. *Hokkaido shūjikan ronkō*. Tokyo: Kōbundō, pp. 339–367.
Misu, T. 1994, *Kushiro shūjikan*. Kushiro: Misu Tatsuo.
Nakamura, M. 1998, *Rōdōsha to nōmin: Nihon kindai wo sasaeta hitobito*. Tokyo: Shōgakkan.
Nasu, K. 1987, *Sorachi shūjikan no shokuseikatsu*. Iwamizawa: Hokkaido shinbunsha.
Ōe, T. ed. 1952, *Abashiri keimusho enkakushi*. Abashiri: Abashiri keimusho shokuinkai.
SBEK= *Sorachi bunkan enkaku ki*. 1993 [1891]. In ASHK = Asahikawa shishi henshū kaigi. ed. 6. *Shūjikan (kangokuho) shiryō*. Asahikawa: Asahikawa shishi henshū kai-gi, pp. 553–627.
SECH= *Shūjikan enkaku chō* 1993 [1891]. In ASHK = Asahikawa shishi henshū kaigi. ed. 6. *Shūjikan (kangokuho) shiryō*. Asahikawa: Asahikawa shishi henshū kai-gi, pp. 349–404.
Shigematsu, K. 1970, *Hokkaido gyō keishi*. Tokyo: Zufu shuppan.
Shigematsu, K. 1985, *Zukan Nihon no kangokushi*. Tokyo: Yūzankaku shuppan.
Shōbunsha, ed. 2001, *Hokkaido dō ro chizu*. Tokyo and Osaka: Shōbunsha.
Yamada, Y. 1997, Hokkaido shūjikan shi. In Takashio, H. and Nakayama, K. eds. *Hokkaido shūjikan ronkō*. Tokyo: Kōbundō, pp. 167–291.
Yamaya, I. 1982, *Abashiri keimusho*. Sapporo: Hokkaido shinbunsha.

5 Conclusion

Given the history of the use of prison labour on Hokkaido from 1881 to 1894 as described in the central section of this book, it is now possible to return to the questions posed at the beginning. The first question concerned why three central prisons (*shūjikan*) and their branches were built on Hokkaido, and if a connection could be found between the colonization process and the dynamics of prison labour use. My data highlight that contemporary politicians shared a conviction that the construction of prisons on the northernmost island would provide a remedy for different problems, all relating to the social transformations experienced during the Meiji Restoration and the building of the Japanese Empire through the colonization of Hokkaido. The first of these issues was the growing mass of political prisoners who could be exiled to Hokkaido, at the extreme periphery of the country, far removed from the centres of political unrest in southern Japan. Importantly, the establishment of prisons suited the Meiji government's colonization policy in Hokkaido, especially in terms of economic development, borderland security and demographic growth. Prison labour could be exploited for the acceleration of the northern island's economic development and the establishment of prisons would populate Japan's northern frontier with Russia. Moreover, the Meiji government speculated on the future settlement of released convicts in Hokkaido and the accompanying population growth in this sparsely populated region.

My analysis suggests that the use of prison labour was largely shaped by the dynamics of the colonization process in Hokkaido. During the first phase of forced labour, from 1881 to 1886, prisoners were almost exclusively used for agricultural and industrial tasks related to rural development. While the prison inmates initially contributed to the rural development process as farmers and craftsmen, this role changed abruptly with the establishment of the Hokkaido-chō in 1886. The political priorities of the new local government focused on the successful recruitment of farmers as voluntary immigrants on the one hand, and the intensification of capital imports to

Hokkaido on the other hand. The large number of prison labourers guaranteed the provision of the cheapest possible workforce, thus making investments in Hokkaido more attractive. In 1886, the administration of these central prisons was transferred from the Ministry of the Interior to the Hokkaido-chō and hundreds of prisoners were put to work in the industrial sector. Prison labourers enabled the settlement of the northeast through the construction of the Central Highway, as well as making possible the military stations situated there. When the Sino-Japanese War led to renewed labour shortages in the agricultural sector, the construction of Tokachi Prison made the rapid development of the Tokachi region possible by providing forced labourers. All of these industrial and road construction activities, along with the return to agricultural labour, were in concordance with the priorities of the Hokkaido-chō's colonization policies. The possibility of a connection between the deployment of prison labour and the colonization of Hokkaido can therefore be unequivocally confirmed.

In terms of my second question, about the type and degree of the prison labourers' contribution to the colonization of Hokkaido, I concluded that the contributions of convict labourers can be summarized into three main aspects: firstly, the preparation for and assistance to settlers; secondly, the construction of a military infrastructure; and thirdly, the employment of prisoners by state institutions and private companies.

This study shows that the prison institutions developed together with their surrounding communities, particularly in the early years of the prisons from 1881 to 1886. The focus of labour on agriculture and craftsmanship during this time can of course be explained by the needs of the prison institutions themselves, which were still in the midst of development. It must nevertheless be noted that the majority of the land developed through prison labour was sold to settlement associations which distributed the land to colonists. Products crafted by convicts were also sold to private persons and settlers could order prisoner craftsmen to carry out various tasks around their houses. Due to the radical shift in prison labour use in 1886 and to the advanced development of the towns and villages, the need for this type of assistance subsided over the years, although it did not dissipate entirely. Rural development by convicts also experienced renewed significance with the halt of all external heavy prison labour in 1894.

The second focus of prison labour assignments can be found in the establishment of a base for military affairs. The accomplishments of the forced labourers here include the building of several hundred living quarters for the colonial militia and the construction of the first Central Highway. The road served the settlement of the northeast, thus enabling the military securement of Japan's national border with Russia and which would play a crucial role many years later during the Russo-Japanese War in 1904–1905.

Thirdly, public and private businesses alike made ample use of the prisons' inexpensive source of convict labour. During the years 1886–1894, an annual average of 1,000 prisoners were put to work in the coal mines of Horonai. The coal produced there supplied not only the Japanese market but was also shipped abroad. By keeping production costs extremely low through the use of convict labour, it was possible, for example, for the Mitsui Corporation to successfully compete with British coal exporters on the Asian market. Yasuda Zenjirō was also able to rely on the cheapest possible labour force when he took over the sulphur mine in Atosanupuri in 1877. In both the sulphur mine and Yasuda's refinery, almost all of the workers were prison labourers. In addition to these two prominent examples, the match factory owned by the entrepreneur Yamada also made productive use of the Abashiri convicts.

The three focal points listed above – colonial settlement assistance, the construction of a military infrastructure, and recruitment of forced labourers in industry – are proof that prison labour was of local, national and international significance during the colonization of Hokkaido and thus the building of the Japanese Empire.

The findings of this study further add to Meiji historiography. I discussed the institutional antecedents of the modern prison in Japan, namely arrest houses and forced labour camps. The principles of confinement and forced labour gradually intersected and evolved into the shape of the "modern" prison. Examples from Edo, the geographical centre of Tokugawa Japan, as well as the geographical periphery in Ezo suggest that these developments were under way long before the "opening of Japan" in the 19th century. Moreover, this study of prisons and forced labour during the colonization of Hokkaido draws attention to the role of prisoners as unwitting agents of colonial processes and empire building. The focus on convict labour emphasizes the role of marginalized, "subaltern" people in the making of history and thus adds an important dimension to our historiographic understanding of the Meiji period and the industrialization of modern Japan.

The book also contributes to the historiography of Ezo and Hokkaido. The empirical findings summarized earlier highlight the ongoing use of Japan's northernmost island of Ezo/Hokkaido as a space of banishment and economic exploitation. Indeed, my discussion of Ezo as a space of exile provides evidence that throughout the colonialization process of Ezo, the island provided central Japan with natural resources extracted under difficult labour conditions and which involved, during the Tokugawa period, the exploitation and sometimes coercion of Ainu labour. After the Meiji Restoration, the Meiji government formalized the colonization process of Hokkaido. Rather than drawing on the indigenous labour force, however, the government opted for the import of labour through an immigration policy.

In addition, the Meiji government decided to accelerate the colonization process through the use of the labour of political and non-political convicts.

This case study of prisons and forced labour during the colonization of Hokkaido also challenges dominant Western theories on prisons as "total institutions". Whilst controllable detention in small cells were common, actual pedagogical concepts did not appear in the Japanese prison system until the late 1890s. In addition, a lack of visible economic output cannot be maintained in the case of the early prisons on Hokkaido; on the contrary, this study provides evidence that it was indeed economic considerations in particular which occasioned the construction of a total of five penal institutions in this region between the years 1881 and 1894, and which determined the employment of prison labour.

Index

lack of cooperation between Edo and 18; Usubetsu in 21
Matsumoto Jūrō 59
meal portions, prison 58
mealtimes, prison 57–58
Meiji government: colonization process 75, 77–78; Hokkaido development plan 5; reforming penal system 29; restricting citizen's rights to freedom of expression 34
Meiji Restoration 1–2, 5
Michishima Michitsune 34–35
military infrastructure 77
miso and soy sauce brewery 44, 47, 48
Mitsui Corporation 60, 61, 77
Miyagi prison 31–32
Mizuno Tadakuni 20
modern prisons 9, 30, 77
morality lessons 58–59

Nagayama Takeshirō 67
Nakano Jirosaburō 35
Nihon Bank 66
Nuppaomanai 49

Ogawa Shigejirō 71
Ōinoue Terusaki 49–50, 62, 64–65, 70, 71, 72–73
Okada Asajirō 61
Okushiri Island 20–21
Ōno Chōshirō 35
"opening of Japan" xiv, 1–2, 77
Oppenheim, Lassa 28

paper production 45
peasant uprisings 31
penal system, modernizing 28–31
political convicts 32, 34–36, 75
potable water 48–49
primitive accumulation 7–8
prisoners: escape attempts of 11, 25–26, 58, 66, 68, 72; fear of 72; future of released 72–73; health of 69; public/private businesses use of 77
prison factory 32
prison labour: in Atosanupuri 63; for economic development 75; exploitation of 75; Ito Hirobumi's views on 56–57; Kaneko's views

on 54–56; from outside to inside 71–73; shaping colonization process 75; wages for 8; widening Kushiro River 63; work uniforms for 58; Yamagata Aritomo's views on 56–57; *see also* forced labour/labourers
prison labour policies 54–57
prison labour sites, conditions of 71
prison reforms 71–73
prison routine 57–59
prisons: history of 7–11; as space of healing 30; *see also* modern prisons
prison staff: children of 47; dress code for 45; at Kabato Prison 43; at Kushiro Prison 51; ratio of inmates to 39
prison work *see* forced labour/labourers

released prisoners 72–73
religious morality lessons 58–59
road construction, using convicts in 55–56
Russia 67
Russo-Japanese war 69, 76

Saigō Takamori 31
Sakhalin Ainu 59
Sandaban Tarō 58
Sanjō Sanetomi 32–33, 46
Satow, Ernest 29
Satsuma Rebellion of 1877 31
sawmill 48
sewing work 44
Shibecha 50–51
Shibetsu estate 40–41
Shigematsu Kazuyoshi 47
Shiranuka labour camp 21
shizuko revolts 31
shoe manufacture 45
Sino-Japanese War 61
smithy 48
Sorachi Prison 34, 46–49, 59
straw-weaving workshop 44–45
Sulphur Mountain, in Atosanupuri 62–64

tailor's workshop 44, 45, 48
Taiwan, Japan's annexation of 3
Takuma, Dan 56

For Product Safety Concerns and Information please contact our
EU representative GPSR@taylorandfrancis.com Taylor & Francis
Verlag GmbH, Kaufingerstraße 24, 80331 München, Germany